Michael Sadgrove has been Dean of Durham since 2003.
A former Dean of Sheffield and Precentor of Coventry
Cathedral, he has also served as a parish priest in north-east
England and as a teacher of biblical studies at a theological
college. He is the author of *A Picture of Faith* (Kevin
Mayhew, 1995), *The Eight Words of Jesus* (SPCK, 2007) and
Wisdom and Ministry (SPCK, 2008). He was born in
London in 1950, is married to a psychotherapist and has four
adult children.

I WILL TRUST IN YOU

A Companion to the Evening Psalms

Michael Sadgrove

First published in Great Britain in 2009

Society for Promoting Christian Knowledge
36 Causton Street
London SW1P 4ST

British Library Cataloguing-in-Publication Data
A catalogue record for this book is available from the British Library

ISBN 978–0–281–05987–4

1 3 5 7 9 10 8 6 4 2

Typeset by Graphicraft Limited, Hong Kong
Printed in Great Britain by Ashford Colour Press

Produced on paper from sustainable forests

*To the boys and gentlemen
of Durham Cathedral Choir
in gratitude for their singing of the Psalms
each evening of the month*

Contents

Contents

Contents

Preface

If it had not been for a better-known author's copyright, I might have called this book *Half the Psalms for Everyone*, which is what it is.

Why yet another book on the Psalms, and why one that begins eccentrically with Psalm 6? The reason is simple. This book is an invitation to read the Psalms as they are set out in the Church of England's Book of Common Prayer. There the Psalms are assigned to each of the thirty mornings and evenings of the month, so that the entire Psalter is read through during the course of daily morning and evening prayer as the month unfolds. This book is a companion to the Evening cycle of Psalms. Hence it covers just half of the Psalter, and begins with the psalms set for the First Evening of the month, which are Psalms 6 to 8.

Those of us who are privileged to worship in cathedrals are familiar with this way of saying or singing the Psalms each day. To choristers and canons alike, the Fifteenth Evening means the longest evening of psalmody in the book; the Twentieth means one of the most beautiful hymns of creation; the Thirteenth means pain and suffering; the Fourth means the homely and familiar Shepherd Psalm; and the Thirtieth Evening means a paean of praise to end the month with. In the introduction, I explain the background to this way of allocating the Psalms and why I believe it still has value.

But this book is not especially for those who worship in cathedrals or who enjoy listening to *Choral Evensong* on BBC Radio 3, though I hope they find value in it. Nor is it written especially for Church of England people. I hope it's 'for everyone' because it sets out to explore the riches of the Psalms for all that they have offered people of faith down the centuries and for the inspiration they continue to provide today to countless people. A way of doing this is to have in one hand the Book of Common Prayer or a modern version of the Bible, and in the other, a book such as this that tries to offer a comprehensive perspective on the Psalms in a short compass. I believe there is a place for thoughtful writing on the Psalms that recognizes their origins in the life of ancient Israel but also suggests how they can help believers in today's world to learn from their insights and live by them. An obvious use for this book would be as a course of a month's daily readings. But it also provides a more general *vade mecum* through the Psalms that, by navigating the 'evening' half of them, encounters their full emotional and spiritual range. If this approach finds favour, another book on the morning Psalms could follow.

The Psalms are one of the world's greatest spiritual treasures. I teach a module on the Psalms in the University of Durham's Department of Theology and Religion and am sometimes asked what I want my students to gain from it. My answer is simple. I want them to *love* the Psalms. This book has the same modest aim. *From the heart: may it go to the heart.*

Michael Sadgrove
Durham Cathedral

Note

---·•·•·---

Biblical quotations are mainly from the New Revised Standard Version of the Bible (NRSV). Occasionally I have provided my own translation of a text. From time to time, I have quoted from the version of the Psalms by Miles Coverdale in the Book of Common Prayer (BCP). However, the reader should be warned that the verse numbers in the BCP are often not the same as those in the NRSV. I had to make a choice for the sake of consistency. So I have followed the NRSV numbering throughout, aware that this may cause a few problems for those using this book in conjunction with the Prayer Book. However, the numbering will only differ by one, or at most two, verses.

When referring to the name of Israel's God, I have opted for the now standard form YHWH rather than the more conjectural *Yahweh* (and the clearly incorrect *Jehovah*). Where this divine name appears in the Hebrew text, it is rendered in the NRSV and most other English translations as 'the LORD' in capitals. The Book of Common Prayer version is not always consistent here, but usually translates the divine name as 'the LORD'.

I have also had to make the difficult decision almost always to refer to psalmists as 'he'. This is simply a convenience and not intended to be gender specific. It does not rule out the possibility – or should it be the probability? – that women feature alongside men as psalmists. To be sure, the Hebrew Bible testifies to a long tradition of women composing and singing songs that are psalms in all but

Note

name (Miriam, Deborah, Hannah). But proliferating *he or she* and *him or her*, let alone the execrable *s/he*, simply makes a text unreadable (as this sentence already is). I apologize.

Introduction

The Book of Psalms is full of heartfelt utterances ... Where else can we find nobler words of joy than in the Psalms of praise or gratitude? In them you see into the hearts of believers as if you were looking at a lovely pleasure-garden or were gazing into heaven. How fair and charming and delightful are the flowers you will find there which grow out of all kinds of beautiful thoughts of God and his grace. Or where can one find more profound, more penitent, more sorrowful words in which to express grief than in the Psalms of lamentation? In these, you see into the hearts of believers as if you were looking at death or gazing into hell, so dark and obscure is the scene rendered by the changing shadows of the wrath of God. So, too, when the Psalms speak of fear or hope, they depict fear and hope more vividly than any painter could do, and with more eloquence than that possessed by the greatest of orators ... Best of all is that these words are used by the faithful in addressing God, for they speak with God in a tone that doubles the force and earnestness of the words themselves. For in the Psalms more than anywhere else they speak from their deepest heart; nowhere else do their words burn and throb and press so urgently as they do here.

(From the Preface to Martin Luther's *Commentary on the Psalms*, cited in John Dillenberger, ed., *Martin Luther: Selections from his writings*, New York: Doubleday, 1961, pp. 39–40)

Many people will echo Luther's tribute to the Psalms. For Christians, they have been central to public worship and personal prayer for the entire history of the Church. They have been at the heart of Jewish spiritual life for centuries longer than that. And among countless others who would not describe themselves as religious people, the Psalms continue to find admirers, for to all who recognize great art, the Psalter is rightly regarded as one of the world's universal books of literature.

This brief introduction can do no more than hint at some of the ways in which the Psalms embody the faith of ancient Israel. But because this book adopts a somewhat unusual approach to the Psalms based on the Book of Common Prayer of the Church of England, we shall begin not with the text of the Hebrew Bible (or Old Testament), but with how the Psalms have been used in the prayer of the Church down the ages.

The Psalms in Christian worship

The centrality of the Psalms in Christian worship was established largely (though not entirely) through their use in the daily services of prayer in the early centuries of the Church's life. This itself went back to the pre-Christian practice of the Jewish synagogue that so heavily influenced the earliest Christians. The celebration of daily prayer took different forms in early Christianity. The so-called 'cathedral office', perhaps meant to echo the Jewish morning and evening Temple sacrifices of each day, consisted of prayers offered in a context of praise and celebration expressed through unchangeable psalm texts such as the *alleluia* Psalms 148–150. By contrast, what became known as the 'monastic office' emphasized the continuous reading of the Scriptures, *lectio continua*, and this involved reciting the entire Psalter according to specific rules during the course of a set period of time. In a pre-literary age, one of the principal monastic disciplines was that monks were required to learn the entire Psalter off by heart. Among the desert fathers of Egypt, it was normal to recite the complete Book of Psalms every day of the year.

In time, this extremely rigorous approach to daily prayer among monks evolved into the less stringent, more achievable requirement that the Psalter should be recited 'only' once each week. The Psalms were to be distributed across the seven 'hours' of prayer during the day and one during the night, an approach inspired by the Psalter itself: 'seven times a day do I praise you', Psalm 119.164; 'I rise before dawn and cry for help', Psalm 119.147. This eightfold path found definitive expression (in the West) in St Benedict's *Rule for Monks* written during the first half of the sixth century. The *Rule*, one of Christianity's great spiritual books, places the divine office, what Benedict called the 'work of God' or *opus Dei*, at the heart of monastic life and spells out in detail which psalms are to be recited at each of the offices in the daily and weekly rhythm of corporate prayer. Indeed, it is not too much to say that, according to the *Rule*, the daily offices consist mainly of psalmody adorned with texts drawn from other parts of the Scriptures, as if there could be no better way of worshipping God than in his own words. 'At these times therefore let us sing the praises of our Creator for the judgments of his justice.'

The presumption that psalmody lies at the very heart of daily prayer has been accepted by most Christians ever since, though they have interpreted it in different ways. In the Church of England, the Book of Common Prayer of 1662, drawing on the earlier prayer books of the Reformation period, retained the principle of the regular, rhythmical recital of Psalms as lying at the heart of the offices of Morning and Evening Prayer. However, in an age when the monasteries were no more, and with the needs of secular clergy in their parishes primarily in mind, the Prayer Book relaxed the Benedictine requirement to recite the Psalter every week, and instead provided for a monthly cycle. All the Psalms were to be said or sung *seriatim*, one after the other in continuous rotation, beginning with Psalm 1 at Morning

Prayer on the first day of each month, and ending with Psalm 150 at Evening Prayer on the last day. All the Psalms were thus allocated to one of the thirty mornings or evenings of the month. (When the month had thirty-one days, the Psalms for the thirtieth day were to be repeated.) The version to be used was that still printed in copies of the Book of Common Prayer (BCP). This skilful translation by the English Reformer Miles Coverdale has stood the test of time extraordinarily well, both for its understanding of the Hebrew text, and for its sensitivity to the 'rhythms and cadences' of spoken English.

While new approaches to the daily office lectionary (which sets out how the Bible and the Psalms are to be read systematically during the course of the year) have relaxed the monthly BCP pattern even further, a number of cathedrals still keep it alive as part of their way of honouring a quintessentially English tradition. In the days when cathedral choral foundations sang both the services of Matins and Evensong each day, the entire Psalter would be sung. Today, only Evensong is sung daily in cathedrals and some colleges and 'greater churches', though Morning Prayer is of course still said each day. So where the 30-day Psalm cycle of the Book of Common Prayer is followed, whether it is said or sung, a long tradition is being observed. It is this way of using the Psalms that has inspired the present book.

At this point we need to say something about how the Psalms have been and continue to be sung. The entire daily office in the medieval western rite was chanted in various ways, not all of which are yet fully understood. However, by far the most important was the way of singing that came to be known as 'Gregorian chant', named after Pope Gregory the Great (*c.*540–604). He was thought to have established its position in the monasteries, though pious medieval folk-memory ascribed its origins to no less a person than the mighty King David himself, the patron of psalmody. In fact, the origins of Gregorian chant are complex and extend over many centuries. But we know that by the high Middle Ages it had evolved into an elaborate system of collective singing governed by strict rules.

Elaborated into eight tones or 'modes', its grammar of intonation–recitation–cadence in the first phrase (or half-verse), a pause at the 'colon' in the middle of the verse, and recitation–cadence in the second phrase meant that the Psalms were recited according to clear principles. The pause in mid-verse, still often observed even when the Psalms are recited rather than chanted, reflects the 'parallelism' of Hebrew poetry. This is clear even in English translation. Each verse normally has a dual structure, with the second half repeating in different words, or building upon, or contrasting with, that of the first. Plainchant also respected the subtle speech-rhythms of Hebrew poetry. The close attention given by medieval theologians to plainchant's theological and metaphysical 'meanings' as reflecting the harmonies of the cosmos shows how important a place the Psalms occupied in medieval worship.

The Reformation introduced a new and distinctively Protestant tradition, that of the 'metrical psalm'. This rendering of the Psalms as lyric poems followed the rules of poetry in the vernacular language, whether for example French, German or English. The requirements of rhyme and metre made them easy to remember, though they were not always very exact translations of the original – and not always distinguished as poetry in their own right either. Metrical psalmody was pioneered in Geneva with the 50 psalms published by Clement Marot in 1543, followed in Britain by the work of Sternhold and Hopkins in 1549, the *Scottish Psalter* of 1562 and, perhaps most famously, *A New Version of the Psalms of David* by Tate and Brady, 1696, often annexed to copies of the Prayer Book. Here lie the origins of English hymnody which has continued to derive much inspiration from the Psalms. We think of 'O God our help in ages past' (Psalm 90), 'The LORD's my Shepherd' and 'The King of Love my Shepherd is' (Psalm 23), 'As pants the hart for cooling streams' (Psalm 42), 'The spacious firmament on high' (Psalm 19), 'O worship the King' (Psalm 104) and many others.

Anglicanism, however, always preferred the older way of chanting psalms, hence the provision of a Psalter in the Book of Common Prayer that could claim to be a true translation of the original as well as a version fit for public recitation and singing. The familiar 'Anglican chant' evolved as a seventeenth- and eighteenth-century development of plainchant. Its shape drew directly on plainchant's respect for the parallelism of Hebrew poetry with its clear division of the verse into two halves. It also preserved speech-rhythms through a system of 'pointing' whereby a change in the reciting note corresponded to the stressed syllables of the text, though sometimes the careless 'pointing' of the Psalter led to habits of chanting Psalms that were rigidly four-square rather than free and flowing as the poetry required. Anglican chant largely abandoned the old Psalm tones for the more modern 'diatonic' system of keys in the major or minor.

This is how the Psalms are still sung in most cathedral services today. But the last century has seen many new developments in psalm-singing. 'Responsorial' approaches to psalmody often draw on the plainchant tradition but make it more accessible by allowing the community to sing an unvarying response to the verses sung by a cantor or small choral group. The Taizé Community in Burgundy has developed easily memorized chants whose repetition, some-times twenty or thirty times with a descant or instrumental elaboration weaving in and out of the basic melody, provide a powerful mantra-like aid to meditation. While hymns based on Psalm texts continue to be written, many 'worship songs' in the idiom of contemporary popular music have also been inspired by the Psalms. And the medieval Gregorian tradition itself has been significantly renewed by the inspirational work of monks at Solesmes and Santo Domingo de Silos whose plainchant CD shot to the top of the charts in the 1990s and blazed a trail that others have since followed. In all these ways, psalm-singing is as vital a force in the liturgical and musical life of the Church as it has ever been.

The Psalms in the Bible

In a brief introduction like this, it is impossible to do more than hint at some of the key themes that feature in the Psalms as they appear in the Hebrew Bible. However, the reader who wishes to pursue this rich vein of study will find some suggested reading at the end of this book.

A *psalm* (which is a Greek word) is literally a song accompanied by a stringed instrument. The Hebrew title of the book *T͏ehillim* simply means 'praises', so the Psalms are, collectively, 'The Book of Praises'. We shall see that this is entirely apt theologically, for praise is fundamental to all prayer. However, we shall also find that there are actually more psalms of lament than of praise in the book, and indeed the first two psalms we meet are both laments that come out of the psalmist's experience of pain or trouble of some kind. The term *Psalter* refers to the book as an entity, the collection of psalms we have in the Bible as it now is, often with a particular emphasis on how the book is used in liturgical worship such as is envisaged in the Book of Common Prayer.

The Psalter belongs to the third and final division of the canon (or authorized collection of books) of the Hebrew Bible, the collection known as the *Writings* or *Hagiographa*.

The 150 Psalms of the Hebrew Bible (differently numbered in the Greek and Latin Bibles) are themselves divided into five books which end with Psalms 41, 72, 89, 106 and 150. Perhaps this was intended to imitate the five books of Moses in the Pentateuch, as if here in the Psalms are five books of David 'the sweet psalmist of Israel' (as one translation of 2 Samuel 23.1 touchingly describes the great king). Each of the concluding Psalms in the five books ends with a 'doxology' of praise to mark its conclusion. Psalm 150 can be seen as the culminating doxology that marks not only the end of Book V but the conclusion of the Psalter as the whole.

Who wrote the Psalms? Many of them carry headings that appear to name an author. The first three psalms of the evening cycle (Psalms 6, 7 and 8) are all ascribed to David, as are many others early in the Psalter. These headings are part of the text itself, even though they are only printed in small letters in most Bibles and don't appear at all in the Book of Common Prayer. However, even the Psalter itself does not claim that all the Psalms were written by David. (Psalm 72 is 'of Solomon' and Psalm 90 is 'a prayer of Moses the man of God'.) Most Psalms don't have headings at all. And even the phrase 'of David' can just as well be translated 'for David' or 'about David'. So while maybe one or two Psalms could belong to him (most famously, the Shepherd Psalm 23), most can't safely be associated with any particular person in Israel's history – or even, for that matter, with any particular *period* of her history either. There are only very few Psalms (such as 137) that can be dated with real accuracy.

That's not to say, though, that the background of the Psalms can't be reconstructed with some confidence. Indeed, one of the most fruitful aspects of Psalm-study in the past century has been the extent to which close study of this concise body of poetry has opened up very extensively the landscape of ancient Israel's worship and way of life.

The study began by applying the tools of 'form criticism'. This approach (to any text, not simply biblical writings) asks: what *kind* of literature is this? What is its *genre*? Is it possible to isolate certain entities within a larger body of literature and identify their *type*? To take a New Testament example: the Gospels appear to contain many different kinds of text. There are parables, miracle stories, conflict stories, nativity stories, passages of proclamation and instruction, songs, blessings and curses. All of these are skilfully woven into longer narratives (the Gospels themselves, yet another *genre* in their own right). But all these forms may well have had their own independent life-setting in the Jewish community or the early Christian Church from which the Gospel writers came. So questions emerge like: how did parables (for example) originate? In what kind of settings were such stories told and why? What were they *for*? To explore these issues can immeasurably enrich our understanding not only of how Jesus taught, but also of what the Gospel writers were doing in creating extended narratives out of these different spoken or written forms.

In the same way, when these questions were asked of the Psalter, a means of classifying the Psalms began to emerge. It became clear that there were a number of major 'types' that accounted for a large proportion of the Psalter. Different writers do not always agree about the names of these categories, and there are some disputes as to which are the most important ones. But there is broad agreement that among the principal types are: *hymns of praise* (such as Psalms 8, 150); *personal* or *individual laments* (for example, Psalms 22, 69); *personal* or *individual thanksgivings* (such as Psalm 18); *corporate* or *national laments* (for example, Psalms 74, 137); and *royal psalms* (Psalms 89, 101, for example). In addition, many scholars recognize *wisdom psalms* (for instance, Psalms 37, 49, 73), *corporate thanksgivings* (such as Psalms 65, 67), *Zion psalms* (for example, Psalm 48), *pilgrim psalms* (such as Psalm 84) and a special group of hymns known as *enthronement psalms* (for instance, Psalms 47, 99).

The point is not to make lists for their own sake, nor to straight-jacket every Psalm into one or other category (because a few defy classification, and some flow from one form to another). It's to try to find out, by examining psalms of the same type, what their 'life-setting' might be, as a way of shedding light on how people lived and prayed in ancient Israel. Some of these findings have been startling. For instance, it emerges that the vast majority of the Psalms have their origin in the public worship or 'cult' of the temple or sanctuaries of Israel and Judah. This is obvious enough when we look at the hymns such as Psalm 150 which lists the musical instruments used to accompany the singing of God's praise. And it would not be surprising if the Psalms written in the first-person plural ('we') also originated in public acts of celebration or lament.

But when we probe beneath the surface of the text, it becomes clear that even the Psalms of the first-person singular, the individual laments and thanksgivings, largely belong to temple worship. When, in one of the most famous individual laments, the psalmist says he will praise God 'in the great congregation' and will pay his vows 'before those who fear him' (Psalm 22.25), he is not speaking in metaphors. These are cultic acts that he intends literally. When the next Psalm confidently states, 'I shall dwell in the house of the LORD for ever' (Psalm 23.6, BCP), it means the 'holy place' of the sanctuary where the presence and goodness of God is focused for the believer. These examples could be multiplied almost endlessly. Indeed, some scholars plausibly conjecture that only very few Psalms did *not* once belong to the public worship of the sanctuary (Psalms 1 and 119, for example). These are late in origin and come from an era when the temple had receded in importance, and stress was increasingly laid on the individual's personal prayer and meditation on God's law.

There have been many consequences of this fruitful line of approach. One of the most important has been to recognize the part the human king of Israel played in the nation's worship. As YHWH's anointed 'son' and his representative to the people (see Psalms 2, 89), the monarch was not only seen as the guarantor of the nation's well-being but also the guardian of its sacred space, the temple. He would have taken a leading part in the cult, perhaps presiding over an autumn festival of new year or covenant-renewal in which he ritually symbolized the kingship of YHWH and as a 'priest' to his people underwent rituals that secured the coming of the winter rains and a fruitful harvest as the cycle of the seasons began again. Here, the evidence is partly internal (from the Psalms themselves) and partly external (suggested by contemporary texts from surrounding cultures such as Egypt and Babylon whose monarchs, like all those of the ancient world, also performed key religious functions in the life of their societies). A likely conclusion is that the speaker in many, even most, of the 'I' Psalms is the king himself. This perfectly fits Psalm 23; and it is the only way to make any real sense of Psalm 101.

This brings us back to dating the Psalms. There was a time when the vast majority of the Psalter was ascribed to the era after Judah's return from exile at the end of the sixth century BCE when the temple was rebuilt. The Psalms were called 'The Hymn Book of the Second Temple' and hardly any were reckoned to come from the pre-exilic period. Nowadays that view is obsolete. Form-critical study has confidently established that most of the Psalms belong either to the pre-exilic temple (from the time of David and Solomon onward, 1000–587 BCE) or to the exile itself. Some, indeed, appear to be even older (such as Psalm 29, perhaps originally a Canaanite hymn that, with the name of the deity suitably amended, may have been 'baptized' into the faith of Israel).

We know tantalizingly little about how the Psalms were sung in either the First or Second Temple, though some of the Psalm headings include what appear to be instructions to the singers or to the priests. However, it is important not to think that the Psalms only belonged to one life-setting in history. There is plenty of evidence to show how Psalms have changed in use down the generations. Psalm 89 is a good example of how a psalm began life as a hymn, then had a royal element attached to it, and ended up as a communal lament. This evolution probably took several generations.

In particular, there is one change that all the Psalms have undergone. For we know that whatever the origins of most of the Psalms in cultic worship, they eventually became vehicles for more personal prayer and reflection. This is because cultic worship itself came to an end with the de-struction of the Jewish Temple in AD 70, though the process of learning to use Psalms outside the setting of the temple had begun as far back as the exile when believers were separated from the holy place and had to re-invent themselves as a worshipping, praying community without a sanctuary to resort to: 'how could we sing the LORD's song in a foreign land?' (Psalm 137.4). Psalm 1 seems to have been placed quite deliberately at the threshold of the Psalter, possibly after the rest of the book was complete, as a way of setting the tone. It is an invitation to regard the Psalter as a text for prayer-ful study, to meditate on it and learn to live wisely by its insights. This, of course, is how we have all now come to read the Psalms – as a resource for personal spirituality. Liturgical psalm-singing is still very much alive, as we have seen. But it stands alongside, and does not replace, the intimate and cherished part the Psalms have come to play in personal prayer and spiritual formation.

Part of the Christian reverence for the Psalms is due to their great importance in the New Testament. There, they are the most quoted of all the Old Testament writings, especially in providing 'evidence' for understanding who and what Jesus was. 'Everything written about me in the law, the prophets and the psalms must be fulfilled,' says the risen Jesus at the very end of one of the Gospels (Luke 24.44). Among many examples, the passion narrative in all four Gospels is replete with citations from Psalm laments whose theme of the lonely sufferer protected by God is clearly the lens through which the suffering and death of Jesus is largely interpreted. The last words of Jesus from the cross in the first three Gospels are all quotations from the Psalms (Matthew 27.46, Mark 15.34 quoting Psalm 22; Luke 23.46 quoting Psalm 31). In the same way, the speeches in the early part of the Acts of the Apostles cite a number of 'testimonies' from the Psalms to show how the resurrection, like the cross, was all along intended by God (see, for example, Acts 2.25–36, where Psalms 16 and 110 are both quoted).

The same is true of the array of Psalm texts that are set out in the early chapters of the Letter to the Hebrews to demonstrate the lordship of the glorified Christ over his world (no fewer than the six Psalms 2, 104, 45, 102, 110 and 8 are quoted in the short space of Hebrews 1 and 2). We must also remember that the Psalms are not only cited directly but exert influence on the style of some of the best-known texts of the New Testament. Canticles such as the *Magnificat* (the 'Song of Mary', Luke 1.46–55), and the *Benedictus* (the 'Song of Zechariah', Luke 1.68–79) are directly modelled on the Psalms' way of celebrating the mighty acts of God (such as Psalm 149). The influence of the many Psalms with lines beginning 'blessed are those . . .' or 'happy are those . . .', such as Psalms 1, 37 and 119, can also be felt in such well-known texts as the Beatitudes of the Sermon on the Mount (Matthew 5.3–10).

The Psalms and human life

In the narrow compass of the Psalms, an amazingly rich world is opened up to us, as Martin Luther recognized. So much of the life of ancient Israel is to be found encapsulated in the Psalms, and we have indicated some (a very few) of the key themes. But what makes the Psalms so immediate and accessible to readers like ourselves who live in such a different era is that they give us a perspective on a community wrestling with what it means to practise religious faith in a wide variety of situations. The Psalter is a book where agony and ecstasy (and everything in-between) are laid bare, and this is precisely how we experience human life in society and as individual men and women. The religion of the Psalms is not some carefully choreographed performance: it is the honest testimony of mortals like ourselves living before God in the world.

The Psalter bears witness to life at every level. Its witness to suffering, its bewilderment and despair in the face of human cruelty, its delight in the natural world and its beauty, its insight into the meeting of politics and personal life, its search for stability in a threatening, chaotic world, its celebration of love and goodness – these are familiar to us in the twenty-first century. But we do more than simply 'overhear' an ancient society responding to a multitude of human situations. For it is what shines through the Psalter that is both moving and unforgettable: its unassailable confidence and hope in YHWH the God of Israel who calls his people into a covenant relationship with him and sustains them to the end. And as Israel of old learned to celebrate the gifts given to her through God's invitation of covenant love to become his people, we too come to the Psalms to learn those same lessons of love and loyalty and to embody them in our calling to live as people of faith in our own century.

The journey of ancient Israel is ours too. The Psalms are an invitation to spiritual intelligence.

The Evening cycle of Psalms

Finally, a word about this book. Every lectionary method of allocating portions of Scripture to be read on a day-by-day basis risks imposing an artificial pattern on the flow of the text. Of course, to speak at all of the 'flow' of a collection of once presumably disparate psalms raises questions in itself: some recent scholars have explored the idea that perhaps like Shakespeare's Sonnets, the Psalter is an anthology with a clear shape and 'narrative' of its own. So we can't pretend that Cranmer's monthly cycle that divides the Psalms into 60 separate morning and evening clusters is an altogether 'natural' way of reading them.

But then picking and choosing our favourite Psalms is not a 'natural' way of reading them either. Its danger is that our 'take' on them is coloured by the very preferences which led us to choose them in the first place. The principal virtue of *lectio continua* is that it exposes the reader over time to *all* of the text and not simply to a *part* of it. It is also convenient, achievable, and provides a rhythm that sits well in a liturgical environment where discipline and pattern matter. There is no explicit spiritual or theological 'value' embedded in it. It is the answer to a simple question: how can we read the Psalms systematically in a way that is also practicable?

So this book, organized around the Evening Psalms as they occur in the Book of Common Prayer, is an attempt to get underneath the skin of the Psalter by engaging with all of it and not simply a part of it. To be sure, the Evening cycle gives us such favourites as Psalms 8, 23, 84, 85, 104 and 150, all of them beautiful and rightly loved. But it also faces us with some of the most difficult psalms in the book. No one would place the violent curses of Psalms 59, 83 or 109 on their list of purple passages from the Hebrew Bible. Nor is the darkness and near-despair of psalms like 69, 70 and 142 attractive to those who like their religion to be a pleasant, genial affair. In Psalms 78 and 106, the theme of disaffection and disloyalty and how God deals with it raises hard questions for contemporary faith. The Psalter is indisputably a tough book. It does not make for comfortable reading, and to work through the monthly cycle makes us face this inescapable aspect of the Psalms.

But perhaps the other virtue of reading the Psalms in this way is that it provides a series of 'frames' that highlight how neighbouring psalms can intriguingly inform one another. Scholars have often noticed how one psalm will begin by picking up a verbal cue from its predecessor, something that continuous reading can highlight. Some of these connections are not perhaps conscious in the text, and yet the reader sees them there. This book tries to make the most of this opportunity. For each of Cranmer's mornings and evenings has their own distinctive 'colour': some, like the Thirtieth Evening, are joyful and celebratory, others, like the Seventh, are thoughtful and reflective, others again, like the Thirteenth and the Twenty-ninth, are filled with foreboding. And some make a journey: the First Evening, for example, rises from lament to celebration while the Ninth moves in the opposite direction.

Ultimately, it is not for any commentator to do more than suggest how the text might usefully be read. The literary and spiritual 'work' must be done by the reader him- or herself. But the cycle of the Book of Common Prayer brings us into the distinguished company of men and women who have read, listened to, sung and prayed the Psalms in this very English way month by month for more than four centuries.

That fellowship will have much to teach us. This book is an invitation to join it in a way that it is hoped will be not only informative and intelligent but also deepening and enriching.

1

Hurt, hopeful, human

The First Evening: Psalms 6, 7, 8

———◦•◦———

The First Evening of the month's cycle of Psalms includes one of the greatest and most beautiful psalms of all. Psalm 8 is a song celebrating the majesty of the creation and its Creator, and is rightly admired as one of the Psalter's jewels. However, before we come to it we must travel through the first two of the three psalms set for the day. And while they are much less familiar to most readers, they are actually more typical of the Psalter as a whole.

Psalms 6 and 7 are both personal laments, that is, prayers uttered by an individual man or woman who is undergoing suffering in which only God can help. In Hebrew, the Psalms are known as the 'praises', yet the largest class of Psalms turns out to be not the hymns of praise (like Psalm 8) but the laments of the individual or the community. So we shall encounter a good many laments as we journey through the Psalms. Indeed, of the first fourteen Psalms in the book, only three are not laments. And as we shall see, while laments have much in common in both their spiritual character and their poetic form, it seems that the circumstances that gave rise to the need for lament were very varied. We shall consider the laments of the community later. As for those of the individual sufferer, his or her plight could include sickness, persecution by an enemy, the onset of death, the loss of a loved one, being separated from the place of prayer, betrayal by a friend, being on trial falsely and, not least, a personal sense of hopelessness, guilt or failure. We shall meet all of these predicaments in due course.

The first psalm of the First Evening, *Psalm 6*, appears to be a prayer for healing in sickness. It's impossible to be certain: one of the aspects of the laments we shall notice is how often very general language is used to describe the psalmist's suffering or 'complaint', and it is often difficult to be specific about the ordeal itself. So while in Psalm 6 the psalmist prays for healing (2) and asks that his life might be spared (4–5), the passionate outpouring of grief that follows (6–7) is connected with his 'foes' (7) who remain very much in the picture in the rest of the psalm.

This psalm introduces us to one of the most characteristic and beautiful features of the laments. It is the way in which the psalmist holds to an indomitable belief that it is *worth* praying to YHWH even in times of pain and suffering. We shall frequently use the phrase 'certainty of hearing' to describe this powerful conviction that God cares enough about suffering to listen and respond to the prayer of the psalmist. Here, as in most of the laments, there is a clear sense that the psalmist turns a corner in the course of pouring out his lament. Whereas the psalm began with the desperate plea not to be destroyed by suffering, as it progresses, the shadows begin to be dispersed by the growing conviction that God has promised deliverance, and this can already be anticipated: 'Depart from me, all you workers of evil, for the LORD has heard the sound of my weeping. The LORD has heard my supplication; the LORD accepts my prayer' (8–9). This lament ends on a note of confidence that God has heard, and will act.

Psalm 7 makes a similar journey, but goes even further. Whereas Psalm 6 ended in confidence, Psalm 7 climaxes in an outburst of praise and thanksgiving for the deliverance that is promised (17). In this psalm the ordeal is clearly caused by enemies whose persecution of an innocent sufferer is pictured as both violent and bestial (2). So convinced is the psalmist of the injustice he is undergoing that he takes a solemn vow against himself as a witness to his own innocence (compare this with the self-imprecation of another legendary biblical sufferer in Job 31). What is made clear in this lament and many like it is that the psalmist's suffering is *undeserved*. The laments often put a direct question-mark against the doctrine of 'rewards', popular then and not quite dead even now, according to which the question to ask in the face of suffering is, 'what did I do to deserve this?' This psalm's answer is: nothing at all.

What is the ground of the psalmist's prayer? It is that God rules the world purposefully, and wishes to reinstate in it the moral order with which he endued it at creation. Hence the plea: 'rise up, O Lord, in your anger . . . Let the evil of the wicked come to an end, but establish the righteous, you who test the minds and hearts, O righteous God' (6–11). So the petition of so many laments, that God will deal with the wicked, is not principally motivated by the desire for revenge, but, rather, to see ethical order and divine justice reinstated in the face of the moral chaos induced by evildoers. Hence the psalmist's conviction that God will soon take action unless the wicked change their ways (12); ultimately, they are not so much his own enemies as *God's*. They will reap the consequences of their own actions (16), while the psalmist himself lives on to praise and thank his vindicator, yhwh.

Psalm 7 ends with the psalmist's vow to praise 'the name' of 'the Lord, the Most High'. *Psalm 8* begins (and ends) by extolling that same exalted name: 'O Lord our Sovereign, how majestic is your name in all the earth!' It's a fitting climax to the laments that have gone before, for the ground of the psalmist's prayer has all along been that God is both the Creator and the Ruler of the universe, however much the 'enemy' remains evidence of the forces of disorder and chaos still at work in the world. And while Psalm 8 is an exultant hymn of praise, the enemy is present even here: 'Out of the mouths of babes and infants you have founded a bulwark because of your foes, to silence the enemy and the avenger' (2). In other words, the very act of celebrating the divine beauty and order of the creation, and praising the Creator himself, is what keeps the foe at bay.

The sweep of this psalm is nothing less than the entire cosmos, from the glory that is above the heavens (1, 3) to the teeming life of air, earth and sea (7–8). In the face of this eternal splendour that so dwarfs our little mortal lives, the psalmist's question is both inevitable and natural: 'What is man, that thou art mindful of him, and the son of man that thou visitest him?' (4, BCP). It's a rhetorical question, with the expected answer: nothing at all; a human being is a mere speck of no significance in a vast, magnificent cosmos. And here is where we see the skill of the psalmist at work. For a rhetorical question with its obvious response becomes a real question with an entirely unexpected answer, as if to say: you thought a human being was a nobody in the divine scheme of things. But on the contrary: humanity is the pinnacle of creation, made (just) 'a little lower than the '*elohim*' (the heavenly beings? God himself?) 'and crowned with glory and honour'. *Glory* was the word associated with God at the beginning of the psalm (1). It would be impossible to elevate a human being higher than this.

Psalm 8 closely follows the creation story in the first chapter of the Book of Genesis in spelling out how 'glory and honour' belong to human beings. It lies not in the moral or aesthetic awareness that men and women have, but in the responsibility they carry towards the rest of creation: 'You have given them dominion over the works of your hands; you have put all things under their feet' (6). This is what Genesis means by saying that human beings are created in God's image. God as Creator has placed the world in the care of human beings, who are charged as his representatives to look after it and administer it. It is an awesome, priestly, responsibility. 'Dominion' has often been used as an excuse to exploit and abuse the delicate fabric of nature. We now recognize that it means the exact opposite: practising reverence for all of life, honouring and cherishing the fragile ecology of this planet we share with all living things. The 'glory' of humanity in our era would indeed be to ensure that our world is bequeathed to our successors as the good and lovely place God made it.

In all three psalms, the enemy is an ever-present threat, both to the individual trying to live out the reality of God's justice in personal life, and to the fabric of the created world itself. At the cosmic and the intimate level, chaos always risks subverting the good order of the Creator. But these psalms also suggest that our response to threat begins with trust, thanksgiving and praise. To acknowledge that God's name is majestic above all else is to walk the path not only of truth and justice but also of safety and protection: for the world, and for ourselves.

2

Enemies all round

The Second Evening: Psalms 12, 13, 14

The Second Evening is an evening of laments. As we have seen, this is how the First Evening began. The first two days of the monthly cycle, both morning and evening, are decidedly downbeat in tone.

Psalms 12 and 13 must be among the least visited in the Psalter. Like Psalm 7, both have as their theme the destructiveness of enemies. In *Psalm 12*, their presence is all but overwhelming. The cry for help with which it opens portrays a solitary believer in a sea of perfidious falsehood, a theme that returns in the closing verse: 'there is no longer anyone who is godly; the faithful have disappeared from humankind' (1); 'on every side the wicked prowl, as vileness is exalted among humankind' (8). This cry of a lonely worshipper shipwrecked on an ocean of apostasy is reminiscent of the prayer of Elijah: ' "I alone am left, and they are seeking my life, to take it away" ' (1 Kings 19.10). The prophet was reassured that he was not after all alone, though it *felt* that way. If the psalmist has any awareness of being part of a community of persevering loyalty to YHWH, his psalm gives no clue to it.

The focus in Psalm 12 is on what enemies *say* rather than *do*, or rather, on the evil purposes accomplished through words that are at once both duplicitous and false. 'They utter lies to each other; with flattering lips and a double heart they speak' (2). The Letter of James graphically likens the

24

tongue to the tiny rudder that can steer a huge galleon, or the little flame that sets a forest ablaze, so wayward and untameable is it (James 3.2ff.). There, the 'double heart' of the psalm is to bless God and at the same time to curse human beings who are made in his image. So the cry for help (1) is a prayer that God will deal with apostates at the point where their evil originates: 'May the LORD cut off all flattering lips . . . those who say, "With our tongues will we prevail; our lips are our own – who is our master?"' (3–4). And, once again, the lament finds its response in the 'certainty of a hearing'. Perhaps verses 5 and 6 are the speech of a prophet or priest in the sanctuary, intervening in the psalmist's prayer to assure him that God is listening. So the psalm can end on a note of defiant confidence in the face of evil, that God's protection is certain. For unlike the easy speeches of the cruel and callous, when God speaks he means what he says. 'The promises of the LORD are promises that are pure' (6).

Psalm 13 is less fiery and impassioned, more forlornly poignant in tone. It begins with a refrain that will become familiar in the laments of the Psalter: 'How long, O LORD? Will you forget me for ever? How long will you hide your face from me?' The four-times repeated *'ad 'anah*, 'how long', gives the plangent beginning of this song a sense of restless sorrow, as if there were no confidence or comfort to be found anywhere. Once again, it is the ascendancy of the foe that gives rise to the complaint, and the appeal to God, 'Give light to my eyes, or I will sleep the sleep of death, and my enemy will say, "I have prevailed"' (3–4). What is implicit in this prayer is that God could not let such a thing happen because not only would it break faith with his 'steadfast love' (5), but it would also have the effect of shaming God before the world. And because the psalmist is confident of a divine hearing, his lament ends with the promise that he will publicly honour the LORD for his goodness by offering a hymn of praise: 'I will sing to the LORD, because he has dealt bountifully with me' (6).

We shall meet *Psalm 14* again, albeit in a slightly different form, on the Tenth Evening, where it reappears as Psalm 53. These 'doublets' are intriguing; among others are Psalm 15 = Psalm 24.3–6, and Psalm 70 = Psalm 40.13–17. Perhaps they reflect how the same psalm, with slight alterations, found its way into different collections before these were combined into the Psalter as we now have it. It's also worth noting that the version of this psalm in the Book of Common Prayer is longer than the text of it in the Hebrew Bible. There it incorporates material drawn from other parts of the Psalter, no doubt influenced by St Paul's quotation of it in Romans 3 (see below), which itself looks back to the Greek version of the Old Testament, the Septuagint, which differs in important respects from the Hebrew.

This psalm reverts to the powerful language of Psalm 12. Its well-known opening line takes up again the theme of human speech: 'The fool hath said in his heart, "There is no God"' (1, BCP). This time, however, corrupt words issue in abominable actions. So comprehensive is the psalmist's experience of evil all around him that not only does he himself not see any evidence of goodness, but the LORD himself, looking 'down from heaven on humankind', fails to discern any sign of wisdom among mortals, any indication that so much as one person might seek after God. Depravity is universal: 'They have all gone astray, they are all alike perverse; there is no one who does good, no, not one' (2–3). Not only is wrongdoing endemic in their disordered moral outlook, it is acted out in their abuse of the righteous faithful, like vultures falling upon their prey: 'who eat up my people as they eat bread' (4). This depressing prospect aptly fits Paul's argument in the early chapters of his Letter to the Romans, where he cites this psalm among others to underline the universal experience of being 'under the power of sin' (Romans 3.10–12).

Who is 'the fool' of this psalm? Not so much someone who is an atheist on intellectual grounds (such a position would not have made sense in the ancient world). Rather, it is the person who lives and behaves as if he or she is not accountable, as if God is not a living, reigning power to be reckoned with in the world. In Psalm 73, it's put as the sceptic's question implying disbelief that a high God *could* know, still less be concerned, about the day-to-day activities of mortals: 'They say, "How can God know? Is there know-ledge in the Most High?"' (Psalm 73.11). This is the Hebrew Bible's familiar distinction between wisdom and folly, be-tween those who, as the Psalter starts out by saying, 'delight in the law of the LORD' and those who follow the self-directed path of wickedness (Psalm 1). In the wisdom liter-ature, wisdom means 'the fear of the LORD' (Job 28.20). It is this reverence for God that issues in obedience to his law that the fool in the psalm patently lacks.

The outcome of folly, throughout the Psalter, is that God will put an end to it – sooner or later. Psalm 14 announces that the end of the foolish will be sudden and dramatic when in his time, God vindicates his poor and pious sufferer: 'they shall be in great terror, for God is with the company of the righteous' (5). And vindication, when it comes, will extend beyond the career of the individual worshipper to embrace the entire community of Israel 'when the LORD restores the fortunes of his people' (7).

If we do not pay careful attention to our motives, psalms like these three can foster an unhealthy sense of being a marginalized remnant of loyal believers besieged by a god-less, oppressive majority. These psalms, prayed out of the iron furnace of persecution, probably do not accurately reflect the situation of most readers of this book. However, there are in many places in our world small, fragile communities of Christians for whom this kind of oppression is a daily lived experience. Moreover, there are instances too many to number, not least within our own society, where the weak are exploited by the strong, and the cruel hold sway over the vulnerable.

So one way of praying the psalms of the Second Evening is not to think of ourselves so much as of these others, and to enter into the words of lament in solidarity with all who are victims of every kind of falsehood. To be alongside those without a voice of their own, bearing witness to their suffering and doing what is in our power to deliver them, is precisely what these psalms describe God as doing. As the conclusion to one of the wisdom psalms so movingly puts it: 'The salvation of the righteous cometh of the LORD, who is also their strength in the time of trouble. And the LORD shall stand by them, and save them: he shall deliver them from the ungodly, and shall save them, because they put their trust in him' (Psalm 37.40–41, BCP).

3

A song of victory

The Third Evening: Psalm 18

———•◦•◦•———

Between the laments of the previous and the following evenings, the Third Evening is a welcome paean of celebration. *Psalm 18* is a king's victory song, and one of the most joyful pieces of poetry in the Bible. In the title, it is ascribed to David himself, as it is in 2 Samuel 22 where the psalm is reproduced in its entirety – another example of a 'doublet'. We should not take this at face value. However, the psalm's conclusion, celebrating God's lasting faithfulness towards David and his descendants, shows that this psalm was indelibly associated with the royal dynasty. If the psalm is not necessarily 'Davidic' to the letter, it certainly breathes the warm, passionate and generous spirit of Israel's founder-king who, whatever the vicissitudes of his political and personal fortunes, was always remembered for his deep unwavering love for YHWH his God. So, aptly, it begins where worship and thanksgiving always begin: 'I love you, O LORD, my strength' (1).

It will be helpful to look at this long and complex psalm by sections.

1–6 The king's appeal to God

The answer to lament is thanksgiving. We have already seen how lament in the Psalms is not an unredeemed state that is mired in sorrow and despair, but rather tends to be a dynamic movement towards a place of trust, confidence and even gratitude (such as in Psalm 13). So, thanksgiving is the spiritual and theological outworking of the certainty that the psalmist's prayer has been heard and is being, or will be, answered. Psalm 18 is an early example of the type of psalm known as the 'personal thanksgiving'. As we would expect in psalms like these, the worshipper consciously returns gratitude to God for the deliverance he has been given in answer to the prayer of lament. Very often, as if to remind himself and us of what he has been through, a psalm of thanksgiving will quote from the lament it answers. In this psalm, following the prologue with its pledge to call upon God, the king recalls the prayer he had uttered when faced with the prospect of defeat. It is entirely in tune with the laments we have met so far, including the assurance of being heard: 'The cords of death encompassed me; the torrents of perdition assailed me; the cords of Sheol entangled me; the snares of death confronted me. In my distress I called upon the LORD; to my God I cried for help. From his temple he heard my voice, and my cry to him reached his ears' (4–6).

7–15 The appearance of God

The answer to the king's prayer for help is dramatic. It is couched in the language and imagery of the *theophany*, that is, God's manifestation in splendour and glory to those who seek him. We must link this with the reference to the 'temple' from where God had heard the cry of lament (6). The keen expectation that the prayer and worship of the sanctuary would lead to a disclosure of the divine belonged to the religious culture of every ancient civilization. Israel told stories of how the glorious *shekinah* presence of the LORD had regularly accompanied the Hebrews in their wilderness wanderings, especially when the law was given at Mount

Sinai (see Exodus 19.16ff.). So, here, the divine theophany is recalled in language reminiscent of that terrifying but defining event: the earthquake and fire, cloud and storm are (and this is not to devalue them) familiar metaphors in the Hebrew Bible of the majesty of YHWH as he comes in power to judge and save his people.

16–30 The righteous king is delivered

In a beautiful image, God is said to have 'reached down from on high' to draw his king out of danger, symbolized by the 'mighty waters' (16). It's worth pondering the contrast between God's *reaching* down to rescue the righteous sufferer and, in the previous evening's psalm, how when it comes to the unrighteous God simply '*looks* down' (Psalm 14.2). Here, deliverance is seen as a welcome transfer from an environment of narrow constriction into a 'broad place' (19, cf. 36): a common image of salvation in the Old Testament is that of space in which to flourish and grow. But his deliverance is no arbitrary act of fate. Rather it is the benevolent decision of a God whose relationship with humans is based on justice and loyalty – precisely the principles that had been revealed in the theophany at the holy mountain when the covenant with Israel was established. So, as the psalmist recalls his faithfulness to YHWH, symbolized twice over by the 'cleanness' of his hands, it's in language that is deeply imbued with the *torah* by which he had pledged to live: words like *righteousness, ordinances, statutes* echo the absolute loyalty to God required by the covenant (20–24). The king is to be a lived example of the first principle of the Ten Commandments: 'I am the LORD your God . . . you shall have no other gods before me' (Exodus 20.2). For his part, YHWH too will be loyal, blameless and pure (25–26); indeed, his very perfection is the ground for confidence in those who call upon him for help (30).

31–48 *The king's victory over his enemies*

After the gentler, more reflective mood of the previous section, the furious pace of this most energetic of psalms is resumed as the king tells of his dazzling triumphs. Again, much of the imagery is the familiar rhetoric of victory songs such as those of Moses (Exodus 15) and Deborah (Judges 5) where the warrior God comes to the aid of the armies that trust in him. But this doesn't mean that the psalm is merely imitative pastiche. Rather, we should *expect* that the register of the heroic victory song would inevitably be adopted by the psalmist in the name of David, as if to say, he (alone among the kings) is worthy to join that select band of warrior-heroes to whom Israel owed everything. In the ancient world, this is how greatness was identified. In the words of another royal psalm, parts of which have found their way into this one, 'Blessed be the LORD my rock, who trains my hands for war and my fingers for battle' (Psalm 144.1). Because of his victories, the king's position as supreme was finally established. 'You made me head of the nations . . . As soon as they heard of me they obeyed me . . . Foreigners lost heart, and came trembling out of their strongholds' (43–45). But as the conclusion makes clear, this is not the doing of mortals, but of God (46–48).

49–50 *Conclusion: God's steadfast love for David*

The final affirmation of the psalm, that God 'shows stead-fast love to his anointed, to David and his descendants for ever' (50) is no mere appendix. As we shall see many times over, YHWH's commitment to the Davidic dynasty is a key theme in the Psalter, already celebrated at the threshold of the book in Psalm 2, and elaborated in other psalms, such as Psalm 132. In particular, the failure of God to honour this covenant when the monarchy fell with the Babylonian invasions of the sixth century BCE was to pose a very major theological problem for the faith community of that period. For it was faced with the apparently unanswerable question, how could such a catastrophe have been allowed by YHWH to happen? (See particularly the Seventeenth Evening, whose Psalm 89 is wholly devoted to this theme.) Such thoughts were as far from our psalmist's mind as they could possibly be. But with the hindsight of centuries, and knowing what we do, we are bound to see depths of meaning in 'for ever' that were hidden from the psalmist.

For Christians, reciting this psalm on the third evening of the month, that meaning, of course, is found in Jesus Christ the Son of David. In his resurrection, the vivid imagery of victory over the enemy is elevated to a song of triumph in honour of the one who has overcome death and hell itself. An early Christian tradition was to regard the Psalms as the prayers of Jesus, uttered at significant moments in his career as Saviour of the World. In that spirit of devotion, it's inevitable that one of our ways of reading Psalm 18 is to hear it as the Easter song of the risen LORD recalling the passion and death he suffered, his harrowing of hell and his exaltation to a 'broad place' of glory and honour. In Jesus, indeed, the 'steadfast love' of God is shown not only to him as the obedient Son and King, but also to the new humanity who in him are 'more than conquerors through him who loved us' (Romans 8.37).

4

God's absence, God's presence
The Fourth Evening: Psalms 22, 23

The Fourth Evening begins with absence and ends with presence. The first of its two psalms opens with the most terrible cry of abandonment in the Bible: 'My God, my God, why have you forsaken me?' The second psalm ends with one of the Bible's most precious promises of grace: 'I shall dwell in the house of the LORD for ever' (BCP). Perhaps no two psalms are better known and loved than 22 and 23. The Fourth Evening is undoubtedly one that is especially cherished.

Psalm 22 is the best known of the passion psalms. Like Psalm 69 which we shall come to later on, its depiction of the lonely righteous sufferer proved especially apt when the Gospel writers came to tell the story of Jesus' crucifixion. Both psalms are quarried as a source of texts to illustrate the Passion narrative, most famously, the opening verse of Psalm 22 which is placed on the lips of Jesus by Mark and Matthew as his last word from the cross: *Eloi, Eloi, lema sabachthani* (Matthew 27.46; Mark 15.34). For the evangelists, this bleak cry for help to an absent God perfectly captures the stark dereliction and darkness of Good Friday, the day God turns his face away from the innocent victim of Golgotha.

This psalm, a personal lament, paints a profound picture of pain that is part of a rich literature of suffering in the Hebrew Bible which includes the 'Suffering Servant' Song of

Isaiah 53, the laments of Jeremiah and the Book of Job. The importance of all these texts lies in the recognition that God both knows and cares about human suffering. The plight of the sufferer, *any* sufferer, is not a matter of indifference to him. This was a key insight of Israel's faith that gave it an especial compassion for those in pain. From there, it passed directly into the New Testament and into Christian theology and pastoral practice. In particular, it is the source of a fertile strand in Christian reflection that focuses on the cross as an abiding image of a God who, far from being aloof from passion, knows suffering from within and whose heart of love aches when human beings are in pain.

It is not entirely clear what kind of suffering has given rise to this lament. As so often, the description of the psalmist's pain, while graphic and poignant, is not specific. It could refer to persecution by enemies: 'All who see me mock at me' (7–8); 'Many bulls encircle me' (12); 'dogs are all around me; a company of evildoers encircles me . . . They stare and gloat over me; they divide my clothes among themselves, and for my clothing they cast lots' (16–18). However, it could just as well point to a mortal sickness or the onset of death: 'I am poured out like water, and all my bones are out of joint; my heart is like wax . . . my mouth is dried up like a potsherd, and my tongue sticks to my jaws; you lay me in the dust of death' (14–15).

Whatever the terrible ordeal to which the psalmist is subjected, it leads him to doubt whether God knows about it or is able to help him. In this pit of despair, he is in a bizarre way close to the experience of the 'fool' we have already met in a previous psalm who says in his heart, ' "There is no God" ' (Psalm 14.1); only here, the absence of God is not grounds for recklessness but hopelessness. And this is no passing episode, no momentary failure of faith. The sense of separation from a distant God is invoked in a pitiful refrain no less than three times in the first half of the psalm:

'Why are you so far from helping me, from the words of my groaning?' (1); 'Do not be far from me, for trouble is near and there is no one to help' (11, and compare 19).

But this is not the end of the story. What is so moving about the laments is that the psalmist bothers to pray at all. It's important to note how his prayer begins. It could so easily have been 'O God, O God why have you forsaken me?' The fact that his opening invocation is 'My God, my God' underlines the psalmist's awareness that for all that he is far off, YHWH remains the God of Israel who has covenanted to keep faith with his people. So the psalmist recalls how his ancestors trusted God and were not disappointed (4–5), and how his own experience from the day of his birth has confirmed God's goodness and protection (9–10). So when, at verse 22, the clouds part dramatically and the strong light of praise and thankfulness suddenly breaks through, it is not altogether a surprise. The psalm's confident conclusion is implicit in the belief that despite all appearances, YHWH cannot change his nature. It is in his character not to 'despise or abhor the affliction of the afflicted' nor to 'hide his face' from the sufferer (24). To hear the prayer of lament and to deliver those who cry to him belongs to the very essence of what it is to be Israel's God.

And so wonderful is this facet of his nature that this 'private' story of transformed suffering becomes the 'public' narrative of an entire community. 'I will tell of your name to my brothers and sisters; in the midst of the congregation I will praise you' (22, cf. 25). It's clear from the conclusion of the psalm, with its exhortations to worship God and its promises to pay vows in the presence of the worshipping community, that personal thanksgiving is indelibly linked to public praise. (Indeed, we shall see later on that the same is true of lament, which is to say that in ancient Israel there was no clear dividing line between 'private' and 'public' as there is for us today.) Not only that, but this story of deliverance will expand to include the entire world and its future. 'All the ends of the earth shall remember and turn to the LORD; and all the families of the nations shall worship before him' (27). Generations to come, those yet unborn, will be told of what God has done (30–31). Passion has been transformed into resurrection. Despair has been turned into mission.

Following this triumphant conclusion, *Psalm 23* comes as a gentle rehabilitation into a more 'ordinary' time. Its incomparable image of the divine shepherd tending his sheep is not less beautiful through its familiarity to the Hebrews and to us. In the Old Testament, the shepherd is a common image of royalty, for it was (and always is) the function of a ruler to care for, nurture and protect those for whom he or she is responsible. So, a common complaint among Old Testament prophets is that Israel's kings have been bad shepherds who in serving their own interests rather than those of the people have led them away from the sources of goodness and growth (for instance, Jeremiah 23). By contrast, Jesus is the 'good shepherd' who shows his love by 'laying down his life for the sheep' (John 10.11–18). And this is precisely how YHWH the king of Israel is depicted in the Shepherd Psalm.

The psalm is a song of gentle confidence and trust that we would not be surprised to find at the end of a lament. It is shot through with what we have called 'the certainty of a hearing'. The author has a radiant faith in the abiding presence of God and in his covenanted 'goodness and mercy', and this is what strengthens him for his life's path. Like the previous psalm, this song knows about suffering and danger: the 'valley of the shadow of death' is as dark as the experience described in Psalm 22. The difference is that whereas that author had experienced God as 'far off' and absent, this one never wavers in his belief that God accompanies him even into the depths of pain: 'Even though I walk through the darkest valley, I fear no evil; for you are with me; your rod and your staff – they comfort me' (4).

Who is to say that the author is not King David himself? That can never be established, but here, if anywhere, is a psalm that breathes the spirituality of 'the sweet psalmist of Israel' (2 Samuel 23.1, AV). Certainly, there are many royal associations, not only the shepherd imagery, but also the allusion to enemies and especially to anointing (5). We should not necessarily take these as metaphors: the anointing of kings was seen as a direct defence against the nation's adversaries (see Psalm 2). Moreover, the king's role as guardian of the nation's faith, and David's famous love of and fierce devotion to the sanctuary, makes the conclusion particularly apt: 'I shall dwell in the house of the LORD my whole life long' (6). Once again, the personal and the public belong together, the faith of the individual – king or commoner – and the worship of a people.

This is a psalm that has found a home in the hearts of English-speaking peoples, for whom *Crimond* is as much a part of their identity as *Jerusalem* and the National Anthem. It belongs equally to tragedy as to triumph, to the most public of occasions and to the most intimate. It has been an inspiration and a restorative to generation after generation, as much in the little demands and challenges of every day as in the larger dramas of life. It is hard to imagine Jewish or Christian faith without it. All of spirituality is here in its serene portrayal of life's journey through light and shadow, walked under the protection of the Shepherd of Israel the source of all goodness and mercy. This is the entire Psalter in miniature.

5

Salvation and strength

The Fifth Evening: Psalms 27, 28, 29

———•◆•———

This trio of psalms seems at first sight to be another evening of disparate sentiments: a song of trust, a lament and a hymn of praise. It might seem artificial to try to find a common thread here. Yet as we have seen, the Psalms frequently pick up words and images from their neighbours, and this may offer clues as to why they are arranged as they are. To reflect on the Psalms in groups, as the monthly cycle of the Prayer Book requires, helps us to make connections that are less easy to notice when we study each poem by itself.

The common link here is the idea of 'strength'. Psalm 27 opens with an expression of trust in the LORD who is a 'stronghold', and it ends with a plea the psalmist addresses to himself, 'be strong, and let your heart take courage'. Psalm 28 draws on imagery we have already met in Psalm 18, of God as the 'rock', and concludes by affirming that 'the LORD is my strength' and then that 'the LORD is the strength of his people'. Finally, Psalm 29 concludes a magnificent paean of praise by calling upon YHWH to 'give strength to his people'. Although the Hebrew words used in 28 and 29 are different from 27, the conviction that God may safely be trusted because he is strong in himself and therefore strong to save is carried through the evening.

Psalm 27 picks up where the last psalm the previous day left off; indeed this psalm of confidence and trust is a kind of elaboration of the Shepherd Psalm. There, the royal psalmist had found his strength in knowing that he would 'dwell in the house of the LORD for ever' (Psalm 23.6, BCP). Here, he repeats the sentiment that the temple is the place of security he longs for: 'One thing I asked of the LORD, that will I seek after: to live in the house of the LORD all the days of my life, to behold the beauty of the LORD, and to inquire in his temple' (4). This endearing concept recurs many times in the Psalter, and gives us a feel for how precious to the ancient worshipper was the place that symbolized the presence of God: 'How lovely is your dwelling place' (Psalm 84.1); 'I was glad when they said to me, "Let us go to the house of the LORD"' (Psalm 122.1).

Like Psalm 23, this psalm knows that danger threatens. The well-known opening line, *Dominus illuminatio mea*, suggests that the 'valley of deep darkness' is familiar to the psalmist: 'The LORD is my light and my salvation; whom shall I fear?' (1). Evildoers, adversaries, foes and an entire enemy army (2–3) besiege the psalmist, yet his faith and trust are unshaken, for the temple provides a place of sanctuary and shelter (5) in which strength is restored. From this vantage point, the enemy is diminished and of no account: just as in Psalm 23 God prepares 'a table before me in the presence of my enemies', so here, 'my head is lifted up about my enemies all around me' (6). So powerful is his love of the temple that he thinks of it as a home, where God's care is better even than that of a father and mother (10). So the lament-like prayers for help that punctuate this psalm's soliloquies on fear and faith dissolve into a song of transfigured hope: 'I believe that I shall see the goodness of the LORD in the land of the living' (13–14).

In this poem, we can imagine the king seeking the protection of God's house against the enemy. The same is true of *Psalm 28*, where God is praised as 'the saving refuge of his anointed' (8). This is an explicit reference to the king, the *mashiah* or 'anointed one' of God. Once again, the focus of his cry for help against the enemy is God's 'most holy sanctuary' (2), the only solid ground against the shifting sands of perfidy and evil. Here the threat is more palpable than it was before: we smell the fear of dissolution and chaos that underlies the opening prayer: 'if you are silent to me, I shall be like those who go down to the Pit'. His only recourse is to trust in the just purposes of God for the world that the temple as a place of cosmic order and stability represents: 'Repay them according to their work . . . Because they do not regard the works of the LORD' (3–5). That recognition turns the lament round. The psalmist knows that God has heard (6) and will help (7) and deliver (8). So he ends by praying for those who rely on his leadership and care as Israel's king, the community of the covenant he endearingly calls God's *inheritance* (the 'precious possession' of Exodus 19.5): 'O save your people, and bless your heritage; be their shepherd, and carry them for ever' (9).

In both psalms it's as if we overhear the intimate conversations of an individual worshipper with his God. Perhaps this is an apt place to pause and consider how deeply personal is the piety of psalms such as these. In the psalmist's relationship with God, nothing is held back. This is 'prayer without pretending', for every experience whether of light or shade, of exaltation or despair, of bitterness, resignation or trust is laid bare before the God to whom 'all hearts are open' as the Prayer Book collect puts it. It is true, as Old Testament scholars point out, that the personal laments and thanksgivings are as much part of the public, corporate prayer of the temple as the hymns.

It is also true that in the individual psalms the way in which psalmists describe their ordeals and the deliverance they look for are drawn from a common repertoire of words and images. Nonetheless, there is an authenticity, a genuineness, in these prayers that does not fail to move us even though we are centuries away from their world. Our quest for a spirituality that is as authentic for our own day may well take very different forms. But it can't fail to be inspired by those who have trodden this path before us. To pray the Psalms is to be reminded that their authors are our fellow-travellers. They are 'companions' who break bread with us, whether it is the bread of affliction or of joy.

The final psalm of the trio, *Psalm 29*, breaks into the reflective mood as if to say: when we have contemplated our predicaments and faced them honestly before God, there is still work to do. That work is the task of praise, which is never completed. Our human careers, inevitably large to us, form only a tiny part of the eternal processes of the cosmos. Creation, says this psalm, utters its own hymn of celebration to God: everything cries glory (9). Like Psalm 8, this hymn to the Creator's power puts humanity in context. But whereas that psalm provides an unexpected answer to its own question, 'what are human beings that you are mindful of them?' (4), Psalm 29 serenely ignores that question. Humans do get a look-in at the end (11), so they are not nothing. But until then, the stage is left to the heavenly beings, the waters and forests, mountains and deserts, and to the LORD of glory himself.

Psalm 29 is quite possibly the oldest psalm in the book. It may have originated as a Canaanite hymn to Baal, the god of the storm, before being incorporated into the praises of Israel's God YHWH. Like the theophany of Psalm 18, God appears in terrifying power, and it is this rather than the beauty or intricacy of creation (Psalms 8, 19, 104) that is the reason for summoning the world to worship him. So, while the psalm begins and ends with the LORD subduing the chaotic waters of the primordial flood (3, 10), there is another side to it. The voice of the LORD works to shake and shatter the fabric of the world. Whereas in other psalms, God's hand builds and plants, here it destroys and overthrows (cf. Jeremiah 1.10). It is the universe in all its fury that this psalm celebrates.

Cosmologists tell us that the universe was born in an event of unimaginable violence. Violence attends the birth of galaxies and stars, the engines of our own and whatever other life exists in the cosmos. Even the natural world is 'red in tooth and claw', as Tennyson said. It seems that the price we pay for order, pattern and life itself is that the raw energies of the universe remain essentially untamed and riskily unpredictable. Yet in all this, the psalmist hears 'the voice of the LORD', the same voice that spoke the word of creation at the dawn of time and continues to speak it today (Psalm 33.6).

Overwhelmed by an awesome, chaotic, even frightening, universe, we feel just as defenceless and vulnerable as when we are faced by the human threats of violence or cruelty, persecution or war. Whether we contemplate human or natural disaster, we look for God to bring safety and help. At the end of this hymn, the LORD of power is unexpectedly invoked as the one who gives strength to his people and brings the blessing of peace (11). That last word, *shalom*, brings this hectic psalm to a merciful point of rest. It's the clue to the underlying conviction of all three psalms, which is that safety, or 'peace', flow from the protection and mercy of a God whose care of every sufferer flows from his care of creation itself.

It is not obvious that a seemingly *un*caring universe can be understood in this way. Yet faith learns how to 'read' the book of nature and discern in it the disclosure of larger meanings. This is not to answer doubt and perplexity. But it is to proffer a purposeful way of navigating the puzzling and painful changes and chances of our existence and, through them, of praising God.

6

The happiness of faith

The Sixth Evening: Psalms 32, 33, 34

————◆◆◆————

The Sixth Evening is one of quiet joy. Its centrepiece, Psalm 33, is a fine hymn of praise in honour of God as Creator and Deliverer. In the course of the psalmist's survey of the great works of God he suddenly exclaims: 'Happy is the nation whose God is the LORD, the people whom he has chosen as his heritage!' This echoes the twice-repeated blessing with which the first of these three psalms opens, 'Happy are those whose transgression is forgiven . . . Happy are those to whom the LORD imputes no iniquity' (Psalm 32.1, 2). And in the third psalm, the idea recurs, this time as the psalmist's personal testimony: 'O taste and see that the LORD is good; happy are those who take refuge in him' (Psalm 34.8).

It is not too much to suggest that happiness is one of the defining themes of the Psalter. The opening utterance of the entire book is the first of twenty-three such 'beatitudes' that are found throughout the Psalms: 'Happy are those who do not follow the advice of the wicked, or take the path that sinners tread, or sit in the seat of scoffers; but their delight is in the law of the LORD' (Psalm 1.1, 2). Psalm 1 is one of the latest in the Psalter. We can safely assume that those who brought the psalms together as a collection consciously placed Psalm 1 as a kind of introduction to the book by way of inviting readers to find in the Psalter a guide to happiness and contentment. The message is: consider the Psalms,

44

and discover in them the way of lived faith in YHWH that is the safe path to blessing.

Both the outlying psalms of tonight's triplet are similar in tone to Psalm 1, as indeed is the next psalm in the Evening cycle, Psalm 37. All these are reflective in character, the fruits of the long experience of contemplating life and drawing lessons from its darker side. In Psalm 32, the author considers the issue of sin and forgiveness. In 34, it is deliverance from some kind of trouble or ordeal. In 37, it is his envy of the wicked who continue to flourish while the righteous poor suffer. These are common themes in the wisdom literature of the Hebrew Bible, where happiness is often spoken of as having a right assessment of human life and, in particular, discerning where God is to be found in it.

The happiness of the believer in *Psalm 32* is that of the forgiven sinner. It is the thanksgiving of an individual who believes that his sin has led to the consequence of some un-identified suffering, perhaps illness. 'My body wasted away through my groaning all day long. For day and night your hand was heavy upon me' (3, 4). So the tone of the psalm is rather different from the more famous psalm where the focus is human wrongdoing, Psalm 51. There, the consequences are altogether inward: the desolating experience of guilt, shame and alienation from God. In Psalm 32, however, there is a more straightforward doctrine of 'rewards' according to which the psalmist's sinful behaviour (whatever it was) has led directly to personal crisis and misfortune.

As in many of the thanksgivings, the psalmist recalls the lament he had uttered in his distress. 'Then I acknowledged my sin to you, and I did not hide my iniquity; I said, "I will confess my transgressions to the LORD", and you forgave the guilt of my sin' (5). The 'naming' of wrong is utterly characteristic of Hebrew faith, as it is of Christianity. Psalm 51 calls it 'truth in the inward being' (Psalm 51.6), that is, allowing our inner selves to be places of honest transparency rather than pretence. To practise integrity, throughout the Hebrew Bible, is to accept our condition for what it is and allow God's judgement and truth to do their purifying, healing work. The psalmist learns through his bitter experience that his only recourse is to call upon God to be restored not only to health but to a right relationship with him (6–7). In his restored state he is able once again to see clearly. God will instruct him in the 'way' of goodness and truth (6–8), the only antidote to chaos (9–10), and the only path to true happiness (11).

Psalm 33 is one of the great sequence of creation hymns that begins on the First Evening (Psalm 8). It starts exactly where the previous psalm left off, with an invitation to the righteous to rejoice in the LORD (1). This is only one of a number of verbal links between the psalms. The logic is: it's the sinner of Psalm 32 whose perspective has been restored who is in a position to survey the works of creation and see in them the hand of a good and wise Creator. And because the forgiven wrongdoer has become one of the 'upright' (32.11), he is now able to celebrate the 'upright' word of the LORD (4) that tells of God's covenant love or *hesed* (32.10; 33.5, 22).

This first reference in the psalm to the 'word' (4) is a natural way of speaking about God's *torah* or 'instruction', as we shall see in Psalm 119. But the next section of the psalm gives it a context that is truly infinite in scope. The 'word' turns out to be not only divine instruction to human beings, but the very creative force behind the universe itself. 'By the word of the LORD the heavens were made, and all their host by the breath of his mouth' (6). 'And God said . . .' is the solemn refrain that reverberates through the majestic creation story of Genesis 1, condensed into the poetic utterance 'For he spoke, and it came to be; he commanded, and it stood firm' (9). The connection between these two nuances carried by the 'word' is clear: just as in creation, God institutes an 'order' that subjugates and defeats the chaotic powers represented by the waters (7), so in the *torah* he institutes a moral and spiritual order created in the hearts and lives of people and communities who embrace it. So the manifestation of divine power in the destinies of nations and people (10–18) leads to the only conclusion that is credible. The catena of verbs in the final few verses sums up the responses that befit the subjects of such a sovereign: reverence, hope, faith, joy and trust (18–22).

Psalm 34 distils the journey the psalmist has moved through in these first two psalms. It's a catechetical A to Z in which each verse begins with a different letter of the Hebrew alphabet. This 'acrostic', as this literary device is known, encapsulates what the psalmist wants his readers to understand about God's invitation and our human response. Perhaps he was one of the 'wise' who held positions in the Israelite court with special responsibility to instruct the young who would become the nation's leaders in the future. The didactic tone of this psalm is hard to miss. It recalls many similar passages in the wisdom books such as the Proverbs where an elder educates the young into the ways of insight: 'Come, O children, listen to me; I will teach you the fear of the LORD' (11).

Like the personal laments and thanksgivings, this psalm is strongly autobiographical. The invitation to worship (1–3) comes out of the experience of deliverance from an ordeal (again, unspecified): 'This poor soul cried, and was heard by the LORD, and was saved from every trouble' (6). This personal testimony is enlarged into a universal truth: 'The angel of the LORD encamps around those who fear him, and delivers them' (7). Those who seek the LORD lack nothing they need (10) for God's deliverance is constantly available to the righteous (15–22). Meanwhile, the wicked will receive their just recompense (16), whence the exhortation to avoid evil (13–14) and stay in the life-giving path that means, as so often in the wisdom literature, 'the fear of the LORD' (Job 28.20). For while the righteous may suffer ordeals for a time (19), God's salvation is certain. 'The LORD redeems the life of his servants; none of those who take refuge in him will be condemned' (22).

This psalm, like the first for the evening, raises important questions about the ethics of reward. We shall face these again in the next psalm. However, all three of this evening's psalms rise above a simplistic world-view that says, in effect, that the point of religious faith is to placate a deity and earn blessing by doing what pleases him. The leitmotif of these three songs is that the practice of religion is intended to lead to human happiness and fulfilment. Faith must always have a moral dimension, for this to regain part of the good ordering of the world which the Creator intends. But humanity is never more noble or dignified than when it is blessing God for his goodness. This is where gratitude and contentment are born, and how we inherit the 'blessings' that all three psalms invoke on those who are God's faithful people.

7

Do not fret

The Seventh Evening: Psalm 37

————◆————

Some evenings scale the heights, such as the Twelfth and the Thirtieth. Some plumb the depths, like the Second, the Thirteenth and the Twenty-ninth. Some travel a journey that embraces both, like the Fourth. But the Seventh Evening breathes a calm, even, restful spirit, a quality it shares with the three evenings devoted to Psalm 119, the Twenty-fourth, Twenty-fifth and Twenty-sixth.

Its single psalm belongs to the genre of Hebrew writing known as wisdom literature. We have already met a similar example in Psalm 34. In these psalms, the ideal of the religious believer is the person who has adopted a serene, contemplative outlook on life. Such a man or woman is stable in the face of adversity, and is inwardly prepared to face turbulence with equanimity. Wisdom according to these psalms means having quiet insight into the ebbs and flows of human existence, and discerning what it means to be faithful to God in the midst of them.

Psalm 37 is an acrostic, like Psalm 34, working through the 22 letters of the Hebrew alphabet from *aleph* to *taw*. This time it does this by assigning not one but two verses to each letter so that the first word of each pair of verses begins with the letter in question. A number of psalms take this ABC form; most of them, like 34, 37 and 119, are clearly intended as instruction. This isn't a device to teach youngsters how to write the letters of the alphabet. More likely, it

49

is a mnemonic to help the reader recall the psalm's teaching and make it his or her own, or as we say, to 'learn it by heart' – a phrase full of spiritual resonance beyond its everyday meaning. Perhaps, too, there is a kind of sophisticated playfulness in the acrostic that reminds the reader or hearer that everyone begins the journey of understanding in the same place, having to learn the rudiments or alphabet of insight, and that all, young and old, are under the same tutelage in the school of the LORD.

As we might expect, a psalm that mimics the simplicity of a child's instruction is not laid out as a complex progression of thought. It achieves its depth by a different means, by stating a single straightforward idea and playing with it in different ways. To take a musical analogy, it is not the carefully worked-out argument of a fugue or sonata form, where the interplay of different subjects and their development is what makes the music interesting. Rather, it is more like a theme and variations, an altogether simpler structure that nevertheless allows scope for as much subtlety of colour and shade as the artist is capable of. The effect by the end, especially when this psalm is sung, is that the spirit is soothed and worry and anxiety are laid to rest.

The theme is stated without preamble in the first two double-verses. 'Do not fret because of the wicked; do not be envious of wrongdoers, for they will soon fade like the grass, and wither like the green herb. Trust in the LORD, and do good; so you will live in the land, and enjoy security. Take delight in the LORD, and he will give you the desires of your heart' (1–4). The entire content of the psalm is here: fretfulness because of those who practise evil; envy of their power and success; the belief that their moment will pass; and the psalmist's utter confidence that his piety will be rewarded by God.

This familiar contrast between the righteous and the wicked is beloved of all the wisdom writers. The Psalter opens on this very note, as we have seen (Psalm 1.1–2), where the imagery of dead and evanescent chaff contrasts in the same way with a living, rooted flourishing tree. But the 'theme' with which the psalmist opens contains not a single, or even a double, but a triple antithesis. It is not simply the obvious contrast between two ways of life that is drawn, between 'wrongdoing' and 'doing good'. Nor is it merely the destinies they lead to, fading on the one hand and flourishing on the other. The spiritual challenge for the psalmist is inward. It lies in the domain of his inner attitude as he watches the righteous and the wicked. He can either 'fret' or 'take delight'; he can 'envy' or he can 'trust'. The test is: will his response be 'godly' or 'ungodly'? Will he have faith and hope, or will he be anxious? So the external, age-old conflict between good and evil is internalized in the psalmist's own way of reading things: this too will be either 'godly' or 'ungodly'. And how he responds within himself will have consequences for his own spiritual well-being, his own salvation.

This subtle layering of the psalm's initial theme is followed through the entire poem. In the 'variations', sometimes one layer is uppermost, sometimes another. It's as if the music is capable of an almost infinite variety of inversions and permutations, so that themes that were concealed in the inner parts of the opening statement later emerge into the open as the melody of the treble line or as the music's foundation in the bass. Thus, the 'two ways' of the righteous and the wicked feature in antithetical statements such as: 'The wicked borrow, and do not pay back, but the righteous are generous and keep giving' (21); or 'The mouths of the righteous utter wisdom, and their tongues speak justice . . . [but] the wicked watch for the righteous, and seek to kill them' (30–32).

In parallel we find the contrasting destinies of the godly and the ungodly described: 'Yet a little while, and the wicked will be no more; though you look diligently for their place, they will not be there. But the meek shall inherit the land, and delight in abundant prosperity' (10–11); 'the arms of the wicked shall be broken, but the LORD upholds the righteous' (17). And most famously (or notoriously), 'I have been young and now am old: and yet saw I never the righteous forsaken, nor his seed begging their bread . . . I myself have seen the ungodly in great power, and flourishing like a green bay-tree. I went by and lo, he was gone: I sought him, but his place could nowhere be found' (25, 36–37, BCP). It is true that the psalmist also takes satisfaction from the prospect not only of seeing his enemies punished but of being vindicated in front of them (6, 34), something with which modern readers are justifiably uncomfortable. We shall come back to this trait in the Psalms later on (see the Twenty-eighth Evening, where Psalm 137 offers one of the best-known examples). Perhaps we should simply say for now that what concerns the psalmist is that *God's* justice should be vindicated. His prayer is for the re-establishment of moral order in the world.

So far, so traditional: this kind of teaching is the staple of classic wisdom literature such as we find in the Book of Proverbs. What elevates this psalm above a simple, even naive, exposition of rewards is its focus on the inward attitude of the observer. The presenting issue for the psalmist is *envy* (1, 7). This is familiar to anyone who has ever pondered the inequalities of the world from the wrong side of the wall. What is its antidote? A beautiful cluster of qualities is proposed. First to be introduced is trust, that is, committing our way to the LORD (5) and walking alongside him (23–24), or being still, waiting patiently for him (7, 9, 34) and resorting to him as refuge (39–40). Next comes delight in God and his gifts (4, 11) which we could describe as contentment (16). The ethical life of such a person is variously described as goodness (3, 27), meekness (11), peacefulness (8, 37), generosity (21, 25–26), obedience (31), and blamelessness (37). To some extent these fruits of trust and delight in God are synonyms for one another. But they coalesce into a portrait of the believer that is exquisitely drawn, and that seems to derive from a fundamentally *thankful* outlook on life.

In the flowering of these God-given qualities, we are not far from the New Testament. The eight Beatitudes of the Sermon on the Mount (Matthew 5.3–10) appear to draw extensively on this psalm where those whom Jesus exalts – the poor, the mourners, the meek, the hungry, the merciful, the pure, the peacemakers and the persecuted victims – are all recognizable, often in so many words. The corresponding passage in St Luke even adopts the psalm's antithetical pattern ('Blessed are you . . . ', 'Woe to you . . . ', Luke 6.20–26). This is not surprising, for this kind of meditative psalm deeply coloured the piety of Judaism in the time of Jesus. The radical step Jesus takes is to set it out not only as a pattern of *torah*-obedience, but as the programme of the kingdom that is about to irrupt into the comfortable, unchallenged life of the world. And in so far as it is in Jesus that we see these qualities uniquely lived out in the human being who was totally obedient to God, he is not only the one who proclaims the gospel of the kingdom and invites people to welcome it. He is the embodiment of its true reality. In him we see the words of this psalm made flesh, and glimpse what we too could become.

8

Longing

The Eighth Evening: Psalms 41, 42, 43

———•◆•———

In our journey through the Psalter, the Eighth Evening lies in one of the valleys. Its three psalms are all laments, and though the first begins with the word 'happy' and the last ends with 'hope in God, for I shall again praise him, my help and my God', the undertow of sadness and despondency pulls relentlessly throughout this evening.

Psalm 41 is a cry that comes from someone suffering terrible sickness. So desperate is his plight that hostile onlookers speculate that his death is only a matter of time: 'My enemies wonder in malice when I will die, and my name perish' (5). Their treatment of the psalmist becomes the central focus of his thoughts, an obsession even. He sees their gestures of concern as not simply devoid of compassion, but deviously hypocritical: 'when they come to see me, they utter empty words, while their hearts gather mischief; when they go out, they tell it abroad' (6). Persecution masquerading as kindness is bad enough, though perhaps to be expected among those who could profit by his death, at least to the extent of having something new to talk about.

But the most depressing discovery the psalmist makes on his sickbed is that even the person he thought he could trust is implicated in this hollow charade. 'Even my bosom friend in whom I trusted, who ate of my bread, has lifted the heel against me' (9). We shall meet this false friend again in Psalm 55 where the theme of love betrayed is developed with special poignancy. The Passion narrative sees in Judas Iscariot the terrible fulfilment of this *soi-disant* friend who turns against the one to whom he owed loyalty and betrays him with, of all things, a kiss. Our English word *companion*, like the French *copain*, literally means 'bread-sharer'. In the ancient world, bread-sharing was one of the deepest symbols of intimacy, hospitality and trust. To violate it by an act of treachery was to inflict the worst of all injuries.

The effect of this is that the psalmist now recognizes where true and lasting friendship lies. 'But you, O LORD, be gracious to me' (10). YHWH will not prove false to his promises, a conviction that underlies the confident opening of the psalm with its emphasis on healing and deliverance. The psalmist's assurance that he will be publicly vindicated before his enemies (2) recurs as his prayer to God that they will be repaid for the way they have treated him (10). And whereas he had been ready to be shown that his suffering was the outcome of some wrong he had committed (4), his eventual triumph demonstrates that his inward integrity remains intact, and God is pleased to reward him. 'You have upheld me because of my integrity, and set me in your presence for ever' (12). It's the journey of the righteous sufferer Job in miniature.

The last verse of the psalm is a doxology of praise. 'Blessed be the LORD, the God of Israel, from everlasting to everlasting. Amen and Amen' (13). While it fits the note of confidence with which the lament ends, it has in fact been inserted into the Psalter at this point at some later stage to mark the end of the first of the five divisions of the book. Each of these ends with a similar doxology (see the final verses of Psalms 72, 89 and 106. So the Eighth Evening straddles the boundary between Books I and II of the Psalter, perhaps a trifle uncomfortably, something that is clear from modern translations of the Hebrew Bible, though not from the Book of Common Prayer itself.

Psalms 42 and 43, with which Book II of the Psalter opens, are a single psalm, as is clear from the refrain that begins 'Why are you cast down, O my soul?' that recurs in 42.5, 11 and 43.5. These psalms should be sung without a break and to the same chant. It isn't obvious why the psalm was at some stage broken up into two, any more than we can say with certainty when and why the Psalter was divided into five books. There is another example of a psalm artificially broken up into two in the Morning cycle, for Psalms 9 and 10 also constitute a single (and in that case very long) psalm.

The psalmist's theme in this beautiful lament is his longing for God. The vivid simile with which it begins immediately establishes this psalm as among the most personal and poignant in the book. 'As a deer longs for flowing streams, so my soul longs for you, O God. My soul thirsts for God, for the living God. When shall I come and behold the face of God?' (42.1–2). As a stricken animal looks desperately for the water that will keep it alive, so the psalmist realizes that without God his life is barren and parched, and if he does not soon find God, his very existence is threatened. Like Augustine coming to understand that all desire is ultimately desire for God, the psalmist recognizes the true nature of his hunger and his thirst. So, in tears that seem to flow without end (3) he cries out to the God who has 'forgotten' him (42.9), somehow believing, in a magnificent effort of faith, that though absent, God can still hear and answer, and will send out his light and truth to lead the psalmist back to him (43.3).

However, we mustn't miss what the psalmist is complaining about here. We could easily read this trial of faith and its expected triumph as charting the ups and downs of the psalmist's inward, personal relationship with God. No doubt the psalm has comforted many a depressed believer in this way, and who is to say that it shouldn't? But the lament is quite specific about what has brought the psalmist to this place of darkness and sorrow. It is that he is unable to attend the worship of the temple and, specifically, to go with the crowds to the pilgrim festival. 'These things I remember, as I pour out my soul, how I went with the throng, and led them in procession to the house of God, with glad shouts and songs of thanksgiving, a multitude keeping festival' (42.4). We can't be entirely sure what is preventing him. Illness or injury is one possibility. If so, the stress on 'the enemy' (42.9–10; 43.1–2) suggests that, just as in the previous psalm, there are plenty of hostile people about, maybe with erstwhile friends among them who will not be slow to take advantage of the psalmist's predicament.

To us, it may seem incongruous to make so much of not being able to 'go to church'. That only goes to show how far we have moved away from the Hebrew Bible's idea that to worship together is fundamental to faith in the covenant God. To the Psalms, faith means not simply practising a personal piety but acknowledging publicly as a people how life, history and destiny depends on him. To be cut off from the sanctuary was to be cut off from God's presence in a way that is perhaps inconceivable to us today with our strongly developed sense of the individual and his or her 'own' faith. Yet the idea of the holy place as a symbol of divine presence and human longing has been embedded into most world faiths since ancient times, even if in the West it is now pretty attenuated. It's as if without the 'us' of public pilgrimage, worship and prayer in the holy place, the individual 'I' can never flourish. So Psalm 42/43 is the 'shadow' side of psalms such as 84 where the psalmist celebrates the joy that comes from entering the holy place. Indeed, that psalm's powerfully felt language of longing and fulfilment is very close to tonight's psalm: 'How lovely is your dwelling-place, O LORD of hosts! My soul longs, indeed it faints for the courts of the LORD' (Psalm 84.1–2).

This interplay between the individual and his relationship with his worshipping community is subtly worked out. If his temple and his God are far off, his faith doesn't fail. 'By day the Lord commands his steadfast love, and at night his song is with me, a prayer to the God of my life' (42.8). This personal (and we could say heroic) faith is the ground of his confidence that he will one day be restored to his beloved temple and its worship. This is the theme of his memorable soliloquy (43.5): 'Why are you cast down, O my soul, and why are you disquieted within me? Hope in God, for I shall again praise him, my help and my God.' It is one of the Psalter's most moving utterances. To be able to say with an honesty that can be costly and difficult, 'I can't praise God now, but the time will come when I shall once more be able to' is truly to demonstrate what one eighteenth-century evangelical divine called 'the life, walk and triumph of faith'. As St John puts it, 'this is the victory that overcometh the world, even our faith' (1 John 5.4, AV). And this is precisely, and wonderfully, the faith of the psalmists.

9

Eternity and mortality

The Ninth Evening: Psalms 47, 48, 49

———◆◆◆———

The Ninth Evening makes a long journey. It begins with a resounding handclap of praise, and ends in the grave with the word 'perish'. In between, it embraces both eternity and mortality, drawing an unforgettable contrast between the kingship of the high and living God who reigns for ever, and the transience of human beings whose inescapable destiny is death. And if Psalm 49 invites readers to find wisdom in contemplating death, Psalms 47 and 48 offer the complementary insight that it is as we contemplate God as king that we begin to make sense of our own mortality.

Psalm 47 is one of a group often called *enthronement psalms*, and has much in common with 93 and 96–99. It is possible that these psalms originated as part of an annual autumn festival celebrating the kingship of YHWH, at which the Israelite king was ritually enthroned as a symbol of God's abiding reign. The key phrase is 'God is king!' (8), a ritual shout that acclaimed his triumph over the chaotic forces that threatened to overwhelm the nation, whether natural disaster (the floods of Psalm 93) or, as here, invasion by enemy nations (see also Psalm 2). We can take the acclamation to mean either that God's victory has already happened and is manifest for all to see, or that it is coming and is the hope that sustains the people. When Christians sing this as a proper psalm on Ascension Day, they mean it in both senses. Christ, the risen and victorious king, has already 'gone up with a shout' and now reigns for ever. However, the full realization of his kingship is yet to come, and it is this ultimate hope that runs through the prayer Jesus taught his disciples, 'thy kingdom come; thy will be done on earth as it is in heaven'.

The song of God's heavenly reign is followed by a psalm that celebrates how his kingship is focused in a specific place on earth. *Psalm 48* is a 'Zion psalm' that praises the holy city of Jerusalem as the dwelling place of YHWH and the guarantee that he will be present there to protect and sustain his people (see also Psalms 46, 76 and 87, all Morning psalms). The theme is the stability and beauty of the city that God has established, 'the joy of all the earth' (2). The name Zion at once associates the psalm to the story of David its founder, and, therefore, to the dynasty that reigns there as God's representative to the nation. So, in tune with the previous psalm's confidence that 'God is king over the nations' (47.8), this psalm draws a graphic picture of the futile assaults of kings and nations on this divinely established city (4–7). Because the temple is a visible sign of God's covenant love, the worshipper can be confident of victory over all that represents disorder and chaos, in this instance, the enemy. And in case there is any doubt about this, the psalm concludes with an invitation to pilgrimage around the holy site so that seeing may lead to telling, and the next generation may know that the God of Israel may safely be trusted as a sure defence (3) not only yesterday and today but for ever (12–14).

After two such exuberant outbursts of praise, the final psalm of this trio comes as something of a dose of salts. *Psalm 49* is a wisdom psalm, similar in tone to Psalms 37 and 73. Like them, its theme is how to negotiate life's perplexities with equanimity, insight and understanding, how not to be thrown into turmoil by the contradictions and unfairness of the human condition: why evil is allowed to go unchecked, why goodness is not honoured or rewarded, why the wicked prosper at the expense of the righteous.

Psalm 49 does not answer these questions, for they are unanswerable: the Book of Job makes this painfully clear. However, the psalm does suggest a way of living with them. That way is to consider that however powerful a person is, however successful, however wealthy, it will all count for nothing in the face of death. Everyone, high and low, rich and poor, wise and foolish, is equal when it comes to the grave. No one is advantaged: we can take nothing with us and our reputations will not save us. Twice the bleak refrain returns: 'Man, being in honour, hath no understanding: but is compared unto the beasts that perish' (12, 20, BCP). Death, the great leveller, unpitying, untiring, shepherds his victims down to Sheol, the shadowy place of the dead. So, the psalm offers this crumb of comfort to those at the bottom of the pile, the poor, the victim, the nobody: they, at least, are still alive. 'Do not be afraid when some become rich, when the wealth of their houses increases. For when they die they will carry nothing away . . . Though in their lifetime they count themselves happy . . . they will go to the company of their ancestors, who will never again see the light' (16–19).

If this is comforting, it's a peculiarly tough kind of comfort. Or it would be, were it not for the glimmer of hope that for a moment penetrates the shadows. 'But God will ransom my soul from the power of Sheol, for he will receive me' (15). This is one of those rare moments in the Psalms when belief in an enduring life with God beyond the grave seems to surface. This narrow, precarious shaft of light pierces the gloom for just an instant before being shut off again. But it appears to affirm that a relationship with God is for ever, not simply for the brief span of life in this world. It's not yet a Christian theology of resurrection: there is still a long path to climb before the Old Testament reaches that point. Yet it glimpses a hope of something beyond this life, however tentative. We shall meet it again in Psalm 73, the Psalter's equivalent to Job's triumphant confession of faith in the midst of his terrible ordeals: 'I know that my redeemer liveth . . . and though . . . worms destroy this body, yet in my flesh shall I see God' (Job 19.25–27, AV).

The measured, even resigned, tone of this meditation on life and death is very different from the confidence and joy of its two predecessors. Yet, read as a sequence of psalms on the Ninth Evening of the month, the progression has its own logic. Psalm 47 ends with the beautiful affirmation that 'the powers of the earth belong to God, and he is very highly exalted' (47.10, *Common Worship* version). This is precisely the theme of Psalm 48 with its insistence that the world rulers assault God's city of Zion in vain, because he has established his throne there. The last verse of that psalm appears in the Hebrew to read: 'he shall be our guide until death', that is, 'for evermore'. So this psalm of celebration concludes with a verbal pointer that looks directly towards the big theme of Psalm 49. We could say that to meditate on living and dying as people of faith requires us already to have acknowledged God as king and LORD, both in time and in eternity. On its own, Psalm 49 might lead us into nihilism and despair. Within the context of the Psalter, and read in the light of the two preceding psalms that celebrate God's enthronement over all of life, it feels different. For while it recognizes the deep mystery of what it is to be a human being, and to stand on the edge of the abyss and ponder the enigmas of life and death, it understands how our existence is given meaning in the light of God and his everlasting reign.

And if, knowing what is coming, we listen to the first two psalms in the light of the last one, we are (mercifully) protected from reading into them a kind of naïve triumphalism that is blissfully unaware of the profound questions all thinking human beings ask about life. It is fatally easy to clap our hands and shout 'The LORD is king!' while the wicked go on relentlessly wrecking the lives of the weak, and the powerful abuse the poor and the downtrodden who have no voice of their own unless it is to cry out to God. Nothing is so damaging to the integrity and reputation of religion as a faith that oversimplifies the complexities of things, that is practised in (often wilful) ignorance of what the world is really like. This wonderful trio of psalms gives us a thumbprint of a faith that is both vibrant yet realistic, that is able to question and celebrate at the same time. To pledge our loyalty to our enthroned, exalted Lord, yet not to run away from the inescapable riddles of being human, is wisdom indeed.

10

Friends that fail

The Tenth Evening: Psalms 53, 54, 55

The Tenth Evening plunges us back into the heart of the maelstrom. Once again, the theme is the 'enemy and the avenger' (8.2) who entered the stage on the First Evening and has never been far from the psalmist's thoughts ever since. Sometimes this adversary hovers as a nameless presence on the periphery of the psalmist's vision. Often however, as we have seen, the foe is centre stage, an indisputable and unwelcome fact of the psalmist's life. In tonight's three laments the psalmist faces the assault head-on. And while he may wish that like a dove he could fly away and find respite (55.6–7), the brutal reality is that there is no escape from the terrible ordeal.

It's worth pausing at this point in our journey through the Psalms to think about how prominently the 'enemy' features in the book. One of the merits of reading the Psalms from start to finish in a continuous daily cycle is that we build up a true picture of what kind of texts these truly are. It comes as a surprise that so many of them are laments dominated by the cruel actions of others. But it shouldn't. Victimhood at the hands of the oppressor is a universal human experience. The Psalter describes not only what was true for so many in the ancient world but, tragically, what continues to be true for so many in our contemporary world too. If religious faith is meant to enable us to see things for what they are, then the Psalms ought certainly to help us identify with the cry of those who are the victims of others' inhumanity. They give us a language in which to pray in solidarity with them, and to express our outrage at the violence and injustice meted out to so many who are powerless to defend themselves.

This evening's first two psalms prepare us for the climax of the third. *Psalm 53* is a bitter excoriation of the wicked whose practices demonstrate their reckless disregard for the God to whom they owe accountability. This psalm is virtually identical to Psalm 14, which we met on the Second Evening. However, when we set these texts alongside each other, we notice a key difference. Whereas Psalm 14 uses the name YHWH four times to refer to the Divinity, Psalm 53 simply speaks of *God* throughout. This perhaps reflects how one psalm may have survived in two forms by being preserved in different psalm collections underlying the first two books of the Psalter. The Psalms in Book I, where Psalm 14 belongs, tend to refer to God by the name YHWH, whereas many of those in Book II where we now are prefer the more formal title *God*. Too much should not perhaps be read into this. However, that this lament is repeated in the Psalter underlines how apostasy, abandoning of the way of the covenant, is regarded as the ultimate sin that a human being can commit against his Maker.

Psalm 54 has the classic shape of a lament that moves from the ordeal of the believer to the certainty that God will listen to him. The psalmist begins by crying to God out of his distress and beseeching him to hear the prayer of the sufferer (1–2). He continues by explaining (as if God needed to be told) the cause of his suffering in terms very reminiscent of the previous psalm: 'the insolent have risen against me, the ruthless seek my life; they do not set God before them' (3). However, the answer to the enemy's hubris will turn out to be the decisive act of God himself. God will help him, and his salvation will mean not only his own vindication but also the public humiliation of his enemies (4–5).

In token of this, he pledges that he will celebrate God's deliverance with an act of thanksgiving in the temple (6–7).

Psalm 55 is an elaboration of Psalm 54, made famous by Mendelssohn's setting of it as the motet *Hear my Prayer*. It follows the same lament pattern of entreaty, an account of the enemy's cruelty, confidence that God will hear and deal with the wicked, and an act of trust. However, it is more downbeat than Psalm 54, never quite managing to rise to the major key of thanksgiving with which that psalm ended triumphantly. Because of the nature of the psalmist's ordeal, this is an edgy, unstable psalm in which the promised outcome is never quite realized. It lurches suddenly from desperation to hope and back again, as if the precariousness of the psalmist's confidence reflects his fragile emotional state. That predicament is the disloyalty of a friend. We have already encountered this theme in Psalm 41. Here, however, it is vividly recalled in all its bitter detail.

The psalm doesn't prepare us for what is coming. The 'enemy' is the usual source of trouble (2) and its effect on the psalmist is to paralyse him like a frightened animal. 'Fear and trembling come upon me, and horror overwhelms me' (5). In the choice between fight and flight there is no contest. 'O that I had wings like a dove! I would fly away and be at rest; truly I would flee far away; I would lodge in the wilderness' (6–8). But there is no escape, for in the city, violence and strife are everywhere: 'Day and night they go around it on its walls, and iniquity and trouble are within it; ruin is in its midst; oppression and fraud do not depart from its market-place' (9–11). Elsewhere in the Psalms, for instance Psalm 48, the city is celebrated as a place of divine presence, order and safety. Here, it harbours chaos, danger and above all, threat.

What is shocking on reaching this point in the lament is where the psalmist identifies this breakdown of all that he had come to trust. Even verse 12 keeps us in suspense. 'It is not enemies who taunt me – I could bear that; it is not adversaries who deal insolently with me – I could hide from them' (12). Who then? 'But it is you, my equal, my companion, my familiar friend, with whom I kept pleasant company; we walked in the house of God with the throng' (13–14). And later on, because he can't let the memory go, 'My companion laid hands on a friend and violated a covenant with me with speech smoother than butter, but with a heart set on war; with words that were softer than oil, but in fact were drawn swords' (20–21).

The psalmist is saying that enmity that suddenly manifests itself at the heart of friendship is the worst form of perfidy. You know where you are with an open adversary, where positions are established and battle lines drawn up. But treachery against a covenanted relationship violates all norms and boundaries by throwing into chaos the assumptions on which human beings learn to trust and love one other, especially where love was given divine meaning through a shared religious faith (14). In those circumstances, the landscape of intimacy cannot be read any more: nothing makes any sense. So it is not surprising that the psalmist launches into a bitter imprecation on his false friends in which he wishes death upon them (15), 'for evil is in their homes and in their hearts' – and he did not know it!

Like Psalm 53 where 'God looks down from heaven', this psalm draws comfort from the knowledge that 'God is enthroned from of old' (19). So the psalmist is, for the time being, confident that his ceaseless crying to God 'evening and morning and at noon' will be heard (16–17). And once again, as in the previous psalm, to hear will mean to act. The psalmist will be redeemed unharmed, and the enemy (who 'do not fear God' – another echo of Psalm 53) will be 'humbled'. Yet these shafts of light are soon eclipsed again by the ever-present clouds that harbour threat. The relapse into the painful memory of his betrayal (20–21), a further prayer of confidence (22), another affirmation that God will judge the wicked, and the mere whisper of trust with which the psalm ends, strike a note that remains uncertain and unresolved.

Beyond verse 23, we feel that the psalmist's faith could collapse again at any time. Perhaps this offends our wish for resolution, the happy ending we all want to know the psalmist eventually finds. However, human experience tends not to be like that. Many painful issues remain unresolved all our lives, particularly where intimate relationships are concerned, as in this psalm. Perhaps Psalm 55 could help us not to expect religion to provide easy 'closure' for the dilemmas that confront us. Rather, it could invite us to see faith as a divinely given space in which to take the painful unfinished business that accumulates over a lifetime, and where we learn to live before God in both the light and the shadow. And if, overwhelmed by pain, or the threat of disaster, or the memory of betrayal, all we can manage is the psalmist's final whisper, 'but I will trust in you', the God who is enthroned from of old will assure us that it is enough.

11

The tower

The Eleventh Evening: Psalms 59, 60, 61

———◆◦◆———

Yet more laments. Indeed, all eleven of Psalms 51 to 61 are laments, the longest such series in the Psalter, and this gives the Tenth and Eleventh Days a decidedly sombre character. In all but the first of this series, the theme is the omnipresent enemy. Tonight's three psalms continue in the despondent vein of the previous evening, though light begins to dawn as this trio of laments proceeds.

The enemy in *Psalm 59* is graphically described. 'Each evening they come back, howling like dogs and prowling about the city. There they are, bellowing with their mouths, with sharp swords on their lips – for "Who", they think, "will hear us?"' (6–7, 14). Like Psalm 55, this psalm depicts the city as a place where hostility lurks round every corner; but here, if anything, the predatory actions of the psalmist's enemies is even more calculated. Like feral beasts they 'lie in wait' and 'stir up strife'; they 'run and make ready'; 'they roam about for food, and growl if they do not get their fill' (3, 4, 15). The sense of threat that pervades this psalm reinforces the message that while we may want to think of the city as a civilized and civilizing place, for many it is experienced as an environment not only of deprivation but also of unrelenting fear. The city, in the Psalms as well as in experience, encompasses both the best and the worst that human beings are capable of.

In the colourful language of the Book of Common Prayer, the enemies 'grin like a dog' (6). But God laughs (8). From

69

the divine point of view, the foe is risible, a mere wrinkle on the surface of the planet, which poses no threat to the sovereign God. For the psalmist, of course, it is hardly a laughing matter, but his prayer makes it clear that the laughter of God is not the amusement of a far-off leisured onlooker but the derision of a very present LORD. The prayer for deliverance with which the psalm opens (1–2) is reinforced by the conviction that an ethical God will not stand idly by while the defenceless suffer. On the contrary, he will swiftly right the wrongs inflicted on them in a way that will leave the enemy in no doubt about the God to whom they will need to give account (4–5, 11–13). So the psalm ends with an act of trust in which the secure vocabulary of 'might' and 'strength', 'fortress' and 'refuge' pulls it up from its febrile beginnings to a point of confidence and rest in the God who shows 'steadfast love' (16–17).

These images of safety are carried over into the opening of the next psalm, but here, the bulwarks that protected the people are once again in ruins. *Psalm 60* is the lament of a community bemoaning the enemy who has overrun the land and the God who has abandoned the people. 'O God, you have rejected us, broken our defences; you have been angry; now restore us! You have caused the land to quake; you have torn it open; repair the cracks in it, for it is tottering' (1–2). In the previous psalm, the chaotic world of the sufferer was like being hunted by a pack of wild dogs. Here, the earth itself, normally so stable and trustworthy, has reverted to the chaotic state from which it came at creation. Torn open and reeling uncontrollably, it has become the wayward, disoriented world of the drunkard to whom nothing ever stays in place (3).

In the Hebrew Bible, the cup of wine that the people are forced to drink is a familiar image of divine judgement (see Isaiah 51.17, 22). The psalm leaves open the question of whether the catastrophe that has been visited on the people is a punishment that is deserved. A similar lament, Psalm 137 (see the Twenty-eighth Evening) regards the Babylonian conquest of Judah and the exile of the people as an undeserved calamity. Here, the reference to the 'sanctuary' (6) makes that background less likely, since the Babylonian invasion brought temple worship to a clear end. Nevertheless, whatever historical event lies behind Psalm 60, it, like 137, stands in some contrast with the message of prophets like Jeremiah who insisted that Israel's disasters were the result of her own unfaithfulness in abandoning the covenant of YHWH. These different ways of reading the history of Israel raise the familiar question of whether suffering is deserved punishment for wrongdoing. We have already seen how wisdom psalms like 37 and 49 recognize the importance of that question; and we shall meet it again in Psalm 73.

Psalm 60 takes on the predicament energetically. If God has caused this disaster to happen, he can also reverse the people's fortunes. So the psalm challenges God to act and give a decisive victory (5). In answer to that plea, a voice suddenly intervenes. The speaker is none other than God himself, his words presumably uttered in his name by a prophet (6–8). The list of place names is a lesson in the geography of the land from south (Philistia, Edom, Moab, Judah) to north (Ephraim and Manasseh), from west of the River Jordan (Shechem) to east of it (Succoth, Gilead). But the point is that it is *God's* land, and every corner of it is subject to his kingship, even if for the time being it is trodden down by others such as the present invader. Encouraged by this unambiguous message, the psalmist reasserts his plea for help (9–11) and concludes with a resounding affirmation of confidence: 'With God we shall do valiantly; it is he who will tread down our foes' (12).

Psalm 61 is an altogether quieter piece. It is the lament of a worshipper looking to the temple for protection. Probably he is separated from the sanctuary either by illness (2) or by the actions of an enemy (3). So this psalm is similar to Psalm 42/43 where we saw how the temple was the all-consuming longing of the worshipper cut off from the place and people he loved. In the sacred space where God is present, the psalmist finds shelter and safety (2–3). In this sense of being beyond the reach of an adversary, the worshipper has indeed 'found sanctuary'. These 'hard' images of rock and tower are beautifully balanced by the 'softer', more intimate pictures of being hidden within the divine tent and under divine wings. Here is a psalm that breathes utter faith and trust in the God who promises to defend his people.

Who is this worshipper? Verses 6–7 are a prayer for the human king of Israel, and these strongly suggest that it is the king himself who is acknowledging his dependence on God in this psalm. 'May he be enthroned for ever before God; appoint steadfast love and faithfulness to watch over him!' These covenant words recall God's promise to be faithful to the people through his fidelity to their king as their representative. (This is a theme we shall meet again in Psalm 89 where it is developed at great length.) So this psalm, linking the fortunes of the king to his love of the sanctuary, is close in spirit to Psalm 23, which as we have seen is most naturally to be understood as a royal prayer of trust. That psalm ends (BCP): 'I shall dwell in the house of the LORD for ever.' This one concludes with the same confident hope: 'So I will always sing praises to your name, as I pay my vows day after day' (8).

All three psalms explore the need for trust in God. Psalms 59 and 60, like those of the previous evening, reiterate the lesson that both individuals and societies face ruin if they persist in an attitude of hubris and self-sufficiency (like the 'fool' who says 'there is no God', Psalm 53). It is openness to God and his (often surprising) purposes that marks the difference between folly and wisdom, between apostasy and faithfulness. Whether it is the lonely sufferer besieged by threats (59) or a people coming to terms with national crisis (60), the message is the same. What exalts our humanity, say the psalms, is paradoxically to recognize that there is one who is higher than we are, and to find in him our refuge and protection (61). The transformation that comes when we acknowledge the Creator and discover the dignity of being creatures is nothing short of life-changing.

To see our humanity in this larger and more glorious context is once more to find ourselves and be given back our lives. These psalms are of a piece with the teaching of Jesus: 'those who want to save their life will lose it, and those who lose their life for my sake, and for the sake of the gospel, will save it' (Mark 8.35).

12

The gift of the land

The Twelfth Evening: Psalms 65, 66, 67

———————◆•◆•◆———————

The 'glorious' Twelfth is one of the radiant evenings of the month. As we have seen, it follows a long sequence of laments lightened from time to time by songs of trust. But the constant refrain has been pain and trouble, and the prayer for deliverance. Even if we include the Morning psalms, the note of unambiguous praise has not been heard since Psalm 48. So the Twelfth Evening brings a welcome sense of relief that for a while the sun has broken through the clouds.

The opening and closing psalms of tonight's trio are both thanksgivings that celebrate the goodness of the land as God's gift to his people. The central psalm is a hymn of praise for God's great acts of salvation, past and present. Running through all three is the theme of God's blessing upon his chosen nation and, through them, upon the whole world.

Psalm 65 is a glowing song of harvest. It opens with an act of praise to the God who dwells in Zion, for the temple at Jerusalem was seen as the focus of the people's prayer for well-being. Solomon's prayer at the dedication of the Temple specifically mentions threats to the land's fertility as one of the reasons for which Israel would pray 'towards this place' (1 Kings 8.35ff.). In that prayer, disasters such as famine, blight or the failure of the spring rains are meant to lead the people to acknowledge their sin and seek forgiveness. In the psalm, the themes of God's goodness and a penitent people's forgiveness are once again linked together (3–4); perhaps Solomon's prayer is specifically being recalled here.

The emphasis on Zion must not mislead us as to the true scope of this psalm. Here, Zion is seen not only as the focus of the nation's prayer, but as the symbolic centre of the whole world. 'To you all flesh shall come' (2). Like the prophets of the exile and afterwards, this psalmist believes that Zion is where 'the glory of the LORD shall be revealed, and all flesh shall see it together' (Isaiah 40.5). This universal vision is carried through the next section, where the psalmist addresses God as 'the hope of all the ends of the earth and of the farthest seas' (5), for this is the Creator who established the world on its foundations and put the chaotic waters in their place (6–7). So it is not only Israel but 'those who live at earth's farthest bounds' who are 'awed by your signs' (8).

All this prepares the way for the concluding section in which harvest is celebrated as the abundant proof of God's everlasting care for the human race (9ff.). The logic of this psalm is simple: if God demonstrated his power and goodness by creating the world, the harvest demonstrates how his work of creation continues into the present. 'Thou visitest the earth and blessest it; thou makest it very plenteous . . . Thou crownest the year with thy goodness: and thy clouds drop fatness' (9, 11, BCP). And while there is no doubt a special blessing implied here for the Israelites who saw their land as a divinely given inheritance (see Deuteronomy 26.1–11), the invitation to praise God is not limited to the covenant people. Nothing less than the whole of creation is the recipient of God's overflowing goodness, so much so that even the natural world finds itself joining in the psalmist's song of praise: 'the valleys also stand so thick with corn that they shall laugh and sing' (13, BCP).

Joy has the last word in Psalm 65 and the first word in *Psalm 66*. This is a *Jubilate Deo*, like Psalm 100: 'Make a joyful noise to God, all the earth; sing the glory of his name' (1). Like tonight's first psalm, this one begins by acknowledging that the praise of God is the duty and joy of the whole of creation: 'All the earth worships you; they sing praises to you' (4). The repeated Hebrew word for 'sing' or 'make music' is one of the most cheerful words in the language. It suffuses these opening verses with an unquenchable sense of hope and happiness that is maintained throughout the psalm – not because life is without its difficulties but because God is an ever-present help during them, as we shall see.

After this introduction, the psalm falls into two sections. The first (5–12), written in the first person plural ('we'), recalls how God delivered his people Israel collectively. The second (13–20), in the first person singular ('I'), focuses on his deliverance of an individual, the psalmist, who cried to him for help. The link is the repeated invitation to the faithful to draw near and worship God because of what he has done for the nation as a whole and for this human being personally. 'Come and see what God has done: he is awesome in his deeds among mortals' (5); 'Come and hear, all you who fear God, and I will tell what he has done for me' (16). This, then, is a psalm of *testimony*, or, as we might put it, faith-sharing. It invites other people into the experience of loving and worshipping God – for this is the only adequate way to respond to the story the psalmist tells, and we tell, of how God faithfully delivers those who call on him.

The first testimony is nothing less than the founding story of the nation. The 'awesome deeds' of verse 5 are the events of the exodus whereby God brought the Hebrews out of their oppression in Egypt, across the wilderness with all its threats and temptations, and into a land of promise and freedom. 'He turned the sea into dry land; they passed through the river on foot' (6) – a reference both to the crossing of the Red Sea (or more accurately the 'Sea of Reeds', Exodus 14–15), and to the crossing of the River Jordan to enter the land itself (Joshua 4). This theme recurs frequently in the Psalms, as we shall see (for instance, Psalms 114, 136); to the Israelites, it was as central to their self-understanding and identity as the people of God as the cross and resurrection are to Christians. And although their history has been one of varying fortunes, when at times it did not seem possible that they could survive the onslaught of enemies (9–12), yet they have been kept safe through it all. Now they have come into a 'spacious place' where there is not only room to flourish (a beautiful image of salvation) but the opportunity – indeed the necessity – to testify to God's goodness so that the whole world may hear it.

The second testimony is more personal. Before telling his story, the worshipper promises to praise God in his sanctuary and honour the vows he made when he was in trouble (13–15). We can't tell what that trouble was, only that he called on God and was heard. 'Truly God has listened; he has given heed to the words of my prayer' (19). Indeed, the last part of his testimony (16–20) doesn't dwell on the ordeal at all, only on how God listens to and answers the petition of a sufferer whose integrity is undoubted (18). And within the argument of the psalm, this is true not only of the individual whom God has helped but of his people as a whole, whom one of the prophets describes, in a beautiful parable of parental love, as his own 'son', called out of Egypt to enjoy the privilege of covenant relationship with a loving father (Hosea 11.1). So, the conclusion of the psalmist's personal testimony stands as his conclusion to the entire psalm. Wherever he looks, the evidence points in the same direction. 'Blessed be God, because he has not rejected my prayer or removed his steadfast love from me' (20).

Psalm 67 is a well-known song of thanksgiving, set in the Book of Common Prayer as an alternative to the *Nunc*

Dimittis at Evening Prayer. In a brief space it recaptures themes from the two previous psalms. 'God be merciful unto us and bless us' (1, BCP) continues the thought of blessing and wholesomeness with which Psalm 66 ended. Moreover, the invitation to praise God is addressed to the whole world, as it is in the other psalms. Here, however, it is reinforced by its repetition as a refrain: 'Let the peoples praise you, O God; let all the peoples praise you' (3, 5). This is amplified by a further exhortation that is based on what the psalm has already called God's 'saving power among all nations' (2): 'Let the nations be glad and sing for joy, for you judge the peoples with equity and guide the nations upon earth' (4). What prompts this outburst of joy is the harvest God has given: 'The earth has yielded its increase' (6). What this psalm now looks for is a harvest of righteousness and worship among all the earth's peoples. It opened with the prayer that God's blessing would lead to his way being 'known upon earth' (2). It closes by praying that his blessing will bring the 'ends of the earth' to revere him (7). It's a beautiful *inclusio* that enfolds the psalm with the thought that there is no limit to God's benevolence. The earth is his (Psalm 24), and the scope of his blessing is truly universal.

13

Desperation

The Thirteenth Evening: Psalms 69, 70

By now, not quite halfway through the month, we have met many laments, enough to have become familiar with this type of prayer that is so common in the Psalms. *Psalm 69* is similar to the personal laments we have met so far, though it is one of the longest and most elaborate. But two features make this psalm particularly important. The first is that, like Psalm 22, it is frequently quoted by New Testament writers in connection with the passion and death of Jesus; indeed, these two psalms, more than any other Old Testament text, decisively 'colour' the way the passion narratives of the Gospels are told.

The second feature of this psalm is that, alone in the Psalter, it includes not just some but all of the characteristics that make up the genre we call 'lament'. We have come across each of these characteristics in other psalms, but not all in the same place, not even in Psalm 22. Here, in Psalm 69, we find the *locus classicus* of the personal lament that not only contains all these aspects but sets them out in a particularly clear way. The structure of the psalm, its 'argument', is straightforward and falls into four clear sections. It begins by invoking God's name and setting out the psalmist's distress (1–12). It continues by pleading to God for deliverance (13–21). This is followed by a fierce imprecation upon his enemies (22–29). Finally, the psalmist makes a vow to praise

God when deliverance comes because of the assurance that he has been heard (30–36).

1–12 The psalmist's distress

As in so many laments, the psalmist's predicament is hard to specify, but it clearly focuses on his personal enemies, perhaps the most common cause of complaint in the Psalter. This may be because he has been unjustly accused of theft (4–5), or there may be a more general experience of persecution (7–12; also 13, 18–28) on account of his fervour for God and his temple: 'It is zeal for your house that has consumed me' (9). This 'guardianship' of the sanctuary could well imply that the sufferer is a royal or priestly figure (or both) with responsibility for the temple, for as we have seen, kingship in the ancient world was very closely associated with protecting the sanctuary and its worship. Perhaps the king is depicted here as undergoing humiliation for (or with) his people, either through a temple ritual of abasement, or at the hands of an actual enemy of some kind. The complaint is introduced by the picture of the drowning man (1–3, taken up again in 13–15) being helplessly swallowed up by the uncontained chaotic waters – in so many psalms an image of unimaginable and terrifying danger. It's not clear at this stage whether God will rescue the psalmist or not: his weariness (3) recalls the familiar cry of 'how long' that we met in Psalm 13. And while the psalmist energetically pleads his innocence in reply to his accusers: 'What I did not steal must I now restore?' (4), he is not naïve enough to imagine that his life is untouched by wrongdoing. Even if he is a royal sufferer, he shares in the propensity for sin that is an inevitable part of the human condition (5).

13–21 *The prayer for deliverance*

The psalmist resumes his opening prayer, but now he gives it a new dimension by emphatically recalling the covenant traditions of his faith: 'At an acceptable time, O God, in the abundance of your steadfast love, answer me' (13); 'Answer me, O LORD, for your steadfast love is good' (16). The repetition of the Hebrew word *hesed*, translated 'steadfast love', is striking, for more than any other word it resonates with the long history of God's faithful dealings with Israel ever since he called them out of Egypt to become his people. But we should also notice that each time, this word is linked in the prayer not to 'God' simply but to 'the LORD', that is, to YHWH. This would be significant anywhere. But the fact that it occurs twice in a psalm found in Book II of the Psalter, where, as we have seen, the psalmists tend to prefer the epithet *elohim*, 'God', to the more personal divine name YHWH, is especially striking. For this psalmist, the cry for help is based on YHWH's promise never to abandon those whom he has called into the intimacy of covenant relationship, of which the Davidic king was seen to be the guarantor.

The request for a 'hearing' in 13 becomes more and more insistent as this section unfolds. The repeated imperatives of 16–18 graphically underline the psalmist's increasing desperation: 'answer', 'do not hide', 'make haste', 'draw near', 'redeem', 'set free'. Sometimes prayer needs to be as passionate as this. The 'acceptable time' (13), literally 'the time of your favour', probably refers to temple ceremonies such as daily sacrifice or rituals of mourning when the people came together to seek God's favour. As if to underline his distress, he recapitulates it at the end of this section (19–21), only this time introduced by the poignant 'you know' (an echo of the earlier 'you know my folly', 5). That we always pray to a God who knows our necessities before we ask, as the old collect puts it, is the ground on which all prayer is based. In this psalm, as in the experience of anyone who prays, this is what turns the cry of desperation into the prayer of confident faith.

22–29 A curse upon enemies

We have met similar outbursts of rage in Psalm 58 and will encounter others, notably in Psalms 109 and 137. As we shall see there, it would be a mistake to take these as 'merely' explosions of blind vindictive fury – though even if these were what they are, it would still be impressive that the psalmist is able to be as emotionally honest as this before God. However, underlying imprecations such as these lies a world-view in which divine retribution will one day be exacted because of the wickedness of the enemy. So this is not so much curse as prayer: 'Pour out your indignation upon them, and let your burning anger overtake them' (24); 'Add guilt to their guilt; may they have no acquittal from you' (27). This entire section is no more (or less) than the continuation of the prayer of distress that concludes by taking the psalmist back to where he began: 'But I am lowly and in pain; let your salvation, O God, protect me' (29). So we should hear these imprecations not as thirst for revenge so much as righteous anger against what is wrong and unjust. Seen in this way, far from being contrary to the ethic of covenant love, they are a way of praying for the more just and ordered world anticipated in the final section, where right and wrong are named for what they are and justice is established on the earth. This is not to underestimate the difficulty of verses such as these, but to recognize that sometimes, the discourse of public worship gives us words we would not dare to utter for ourselves. And that can be a relief.

30–36 From plea to praise

The change of tone from lament to thanksgiving is particularly abrupt in this psalm. Perhaps we should imagine a space between verses 29 and 30, the plea of distress and the confidence that help is near. We have seen that even the most personal of psalms have a life-setting in temple worship. So that space was possibly filled by some sudden disclosure of God's presence in the temple (what scholars call a 'theophany'); or maybe by a prophet intervening with a word of reassurance. This cathartic change of mood begins and ends in worship. As in other laments, such as Psalm 22, this one ends not simply with a personal 'certainty of hearing', but with public vows of thanksgiving (30–32). So public are they indeed that nothing less than the whole creation is called to join in blessing God who delivers and saves those who call on him: 'Let heaven and earth praise him, the seas and everything that moves in them' (34).

The theme of this, one of the greatest laments, is that the sufferer in distress is not only *known* by God but is *present* to him. This has special significance for how we read the Passion narrative. At one level it can be seen through the template of the psalm-laments as precisely the story of the archetypal righteous poor man unjustly persecuted by his enemies but ultimately vindicated by God. For the Christian reader, this psalm sets out as clearly as anywhere the movement from death to resurrection that is the story of Jesus and, in him, the story of us all.

And this, in miniature, is the shape of *Psalm 70*. This little psalm may seem just a satellite of its great predecessor. However, it has a claim to fame through its opening verse, well known to centuries of worshippers as one of the opening versicles of the church's daily office: 'O God, make speed to save us: / O LORD, make haste to help us.' (It is true that it has normally been prayed in the plural rather than the singular.) That these familiar words are drawn from a lament is to acknowledge that in prayer, as in every other respect, without God we are helpless or, in the psalm's words, 'poor and needy' (5). Help is a matter of urgency, from the opening plea to 'make haste' to the closing prayer 'do not delay'. But when help comes, need is turned to joy and joy into testimony: 'Let those who love your salvation say evermore, "God is great!"' (4). To be re-humanized in this way, like the prodigal son, and find once again our place before God in the world is one way of defining religion.

14

Bewilderment

The Fourteenth Evening: Psalms 73, 74

————•◆•————

These two psalms seem at first to be very different in character: a wisdom meditation followed by a community lament. But if the first psalm is a quieter, more reflective piece and the second fiery and impassioned, there is a clear connection between them. The link is the question 'why?' with which Psalm 74 begins. In both, the psalmist is seeking to understand events that perplex him. In the first psalm, it is why the wicked succeed and prosper at the expense of the righteous (that is, himself) that bewilders him. In the second, it is why God should allow his holy place to be overrun and destroyed by the enemy. In both psalms, the issue is fundamentally the same. It is the problem of *theodicy* that has engaged the minds of religious people since time immemorial, and continues to exercise people of faith today: how to believe with integrity in a good and wise God in a world that appears to be so arbitrary and capricious.

Psalm 73 is perhaps the greatest of the wisdom psalms; indeed, it is one of the most probing pieces of literature in the Hebrew Bible. Its starting point is the same as Psalm 37, 'Do not fret because of the wicked; do not be envious of wrongdoers.' But it goes far beyond that psalm in its acute psychological and spiritual perception of human nature, not least as a highly personal meditation that autobiographically charts the landscape of the psalmist's own life.

85

The psalm begins with what looks like an orthodox statement of belief: 'Truly God is good to the upright' (or to 'Israel' depending on how we read the Hebrew) (1). Statements like this (perhaps meant to be read in implied quotation marks?) are very easy to make, but the theme of the psalm is to test whether the creedal assertion matches experience. So without further ado, the psalmist launches out on his story. 'As for me, my feet had almost stumbled . . . for I was envious of the arrogant' (2–3). Psalm 37 may warn against futile worry, but here the psalmist could not help himself. The prosperity of the arrogant is described with striking imagery as if the psalmist has personally had his nose rubbed in their graceless affluence. He sees them gliding around 'sound and sleek' (4), wearing their pride like a necklace and violence like clothing (6), a kind of second skin. Porcine eyes bulbous with fat (7), mouths gaping open to the sky and tongues greedily scouring the earth for fodder (9) build up the unpleasant image of a grotesque self-inflated beast – for such people, to the psalmist, have forfeited their right to be called human. And this is the symptom of their deadly underlying disease, the functional atheism we have already met in Psalm 14. Like the fool who says, 'there is no God', they proudly defy their Maker with the question that most characterizes the arrogant: 'How can God know? Is there knowledge in the Most High?' What does a remote, transcendent deity know or care about anything (11)?

After this graphic and colourful portrait of hubris the psalmist returns to his testimony. If the arrogant are so favoured, what is the point of being wise or good or religious – this is the heart of the psalmist's dilemma. 'All in vain have I kept my heart clean and washed my hands in innocence. For all day long I have been plagued, and am punished every morning' (13–14). The inward struggle between the faith of verse 1 and the experience of the following verses is an unbearable burden, for there is simply no answer to this conflict (15–16). The circle of theodicy cannot be squared. Until, that is, the great turning point of this psalm: 'I went into the sanctuary of God' (17). In this life-changing moment, illumination happens; there is a sudden disclosure of how things truly are. 'Then I perceived their end' (17). It's as if the psalmist has been given spectacles so that where previously there had been only hints and nudges of reality, now at last everything comes into focus.

Something very striking happens to the psalmist's discourse here. Up to now, the story has been told in the first and third person: this is how it is with *them*; these are the consequences for *me*. But no sooner has he experienced this sudden reorientation of perspective than he turns to address God himself. 'Truly *you* set them in slippery places; *you* make them fall to ruin' (18, my italics). Narrative turns into prayer, and remains in that mode for the rest of the psalm. In other words, it is as the psalmist turns towards God that everything else begins to make sense. He understands now the truth already sketched out in Psalms 37 and 49 (of which there are many echoes in this psalm). Above all, he recognizes that good fortune is a chimera, an insubstantial dream (20); once seen for what it is, those favoured by it are to be pitied not envied, for it blinds them to the infinitely better, more lasting rewards that the psalmist has now discovered.

What are these rewards? The psalmist likens his earlier, pre-enlightened state to that of a 'brute beast' (22). This creature is *Behemoth*, familiar to us from its affectionate portrayal in the Book of Job. So, while the arrogant had become bestial through their pride and avarice, there had been a comparable risk to the psalmist: that he too would be brutalized through the sin of envy (3). But what he now describes is how the corrupting effects of envy are transfigured by humanizing desire, not for the wealth of the unrighteous but for God. And so the psalm rises to a magnificent climax of faith: 'Nevertheless I am continually with you; you hold my right hand. You guide me with your counsel, and afterwards you will receive me with honour. Whom have I in heaven but you? And there is nothing on earth that I desire other than you. My flesh and my heart may fail, but God is the strength of my heart and my portion for ever' (23–26). This marvellous affirmation is the Psalter's equivalent of Job's triumph of faith in a God who transcends all that time and circumstance bring mortals, whether it is success or suffering.

The psalmist ends with an elaboration of the opening creedal statement, but this time without quotation marks, for the conventional rewards-and-punishment formula he had trotted out has become his personal confession of a lived faith. 'But for me it is good to be near God; I have made the LORD God my refuge, to tell of all your works' (28). He has made the pilgrimage from the *words* of religion to the inward *experience* of it, perhaps the most important journey a human being can ever make.

After this satisfying resolution, the questions return with renewed force in *Psalm 74*. 'O God, *why* do you cast us off for ever? *Why* does your anger smoke against the sheep of your pasture? . . . *How long*, O LORD, is the foe to scoff? . . . *Why* do you hold back your hand . . . ?' (Psalm 74.1, 10, 11, my italics). As in the wisdom poem, faith is on trial again in this passionate, angry psalm, for it seems that despite his promises, God has deserted his temple, his holy city and the people whom he had pledged always to keep as his own possession through the covenant he had made with their ancestors.

Psalm 74 is one of a small number of community laments arising out of national disaster. Among the Evening psalms, there are important examples of this type to come – in

Psalms 89, 106 and 137. This psalm appears to have been written following the invasion of the Babylonians in 587 BCE and the collapse of the kingdom of Judah. It surveys a city and a community whose life is literally and spiritually in ruins, and pleads that God should recall the promises he had made to Israel in past ages: 'Remember your congregation, which you acquired long ago . . . Remember Mount Zion, where you came to dwell' (2). The psalm catalogues the desecration of their holy and beautiful house (4–8), the cherished symbol of divine presence. Even when it has been hacked to pieces by the enemy, its detail is lovingly recalled in a way that echoes the devotion with which the psalmist had celebrated Zion and the Temple in Psalm 48. For now, memory is all that is left to the community. With the destruction of the Temple, it is as if God has fled from his people. 'We do not see our emblems; there is no longer any prophet, and there is no one among us who knows how long' (9).

Baffled and bewildered, the psalmist turns back to the ancient traditions of Israel in a heroic act of faith. Like the great 'until' at the turning point of Psalm 73 (17), this psalm also has its moment of disclosure where the psalmist's night is transfigured by the power of memory. It's a memory more ancient than the Temple or Zion or even the covenant itself, for it takes the psalmist back to the beginning of time. 'Yet God my King is from of old' (12). This confession of faith against all the odds launches the psalmist into a recital of God's mighty acts of creation (12–17). He reminds himself how God's power triumphed over the chaotic forces of the primeval flood, including Leviathan and the 'dragons' of the deep. The thought is not simply that if God is strong enough to vanquish mythological enemies such as these, he is able to overcome the power of Babylon. It is also that what has been reduced to chaos – the land, its temple and its community – can be rebuilt by the God who constructed the cosmos in the beginning with everything good and ordered and knowing its place.

With this transformed vision, the psalm resumes the prayer that God may 'remember' (18) and have regard for the covenant (20). To the psalmist, what ultimately matters is not that the people should be rescued from disaster but that God's own honour should be vindicated (22). It would be too much to claim that this lament ends on a note of hope. However, the final plea that God will 'not forget' the chaotic clamour and uproar of the foe is perhaps uttered not so much in angry desperation as out of the conviction, nourished by the traditions of faith, that God remains the sovereign power of the universe, 'King from of old' (12). In his own time, however 'long' that is, he will come with power, and will act once more.

15

Lessons of history

The Fifteenth Evening: Psalm 78

---·•◆•·---

Psalm 78 is not the longest psalm in the book: it's not even half the length of Psalm 119. But it is the clear runner-up, and the Fifteenth Evening, famously for cathedral choristers, is by far the longest evening of the month. This psalm, with its perspective on Israel's history, offers a grand climax, like a full moon, exactly halfway through the monthly cycle of the Psalms.

To understand why this psalm was written, we should look first at how it begins and ends. The opening section (1–8) sets out the psalmist's programme, which is to tell the story of Israel's past: 'the glorious deeds of the LORD, and his might, and the wonders that he has done' (4). Theologians call this story *Heilsgeschichte*, 'salvation history'. To put it simply, this German word means the distinctive events that have shaped the sacred traditions of the community's faith, and in which God's covenant purposes of justice and mercy have been disclosed. The word *tradition* literally means 'that which is handed on', and in this psalm we see how the psalmist is consciously ensuring that the 'tradition' is kept alive and delivered safely to the next generation, for them in turn to make it their own.

But the 'handing on' of the story is not a matter of rehearsing it mechanically. The tradition remains a life-bearing story only if its lessons are constantly taken to heart as part of the lived experience of the community that is

91

formed by it. This, too, is clear from the prologue. Its opening words straight away recall how the wise in ancient Israel
would summon the young to learn from their instruction
(see Proverbs 1.1–9). 'Give ear, O my people, to my teaching; incline your ears to the words of my mouth' (1). So this
is history with a moral and spiritual purpose. It is to make
sure that the 'next generation', 'children yet unborn' (6) will
'set their hope in God, and not forget the works of God, but
keep his commandments; and that they should not be like
their ancestors, a stubborn and rebellious generation, a generation whose heart was not steadfast, whose spirit was not
faithful to God' (7–8). The intention could not be clearer,
for if this narrative is the tale of God's purposes, it is also
the story of Israel's consistent faithlessness and apostasy. In
this respect, Psalm 78 is very similar to 106.

It is a well-known fact that those who will not learn from
the mistakes of the past are condemned to repeat them in
the present. But this psalm does not simply indulge in the
depressing reminder of the failures of the past. Here we need
to look ahead to where the psalm ends up, for the conclusion is in the psalmist's mind throughout his long narrative.
'He rejected the tent of Joseph, he did not choose the tribe
of Ephraim; but he chose the tribe of Judah, Mount Zion,
which he loves' (67). This is a key statement. It shows that
the psalm originated in the kingdom of Judah whose claims
to be the legitimate heir of God's promise are vigorously
upheld against those of the northern kingdom of Israel (in
the Hebrew Bible often referred to by the old tribal names
of 'Joseph' or 'Ephraim'). Indeed, at one level the psalm is a
diatribe against the false claims of the northern, by now
probably defunct, kingdom whose perfidiousness is consistent with the rebellion of the Hebrews in ages past.

It goes on in extravagant language to exult in Judah's
symbolic and spiritual focus, the temple at Jerusalem, 'like
the high heavens, like the earth, which he has founded

for ever' (69). The claim to legitimacy is unambiguously established through God's choice of King David, a southerner from the tribe of Judah, to reign over his people. 'He chose his servant David, and took him from the sheepfolds; . . . he brought him to be the shepherd of his people Jacob, of Israel, his inheritance' (71). In contrast to the different dynasties that exercised power in the north after its separation from Judah in the tenth century BCE, the south always remained faithful to the memory of its beloved king whose dynasty survived right up to the exile (on this, see Psalm 89). So, despite the strain of disaffection and disloyalty that runs through the psalm, its final verses make it clear that it is after all a celebration of God's promise to establish the kingdom of Judah in its own land. The message is that not even the waywardness of an entire people can thwart that intention.

The psalm follows the broad shape of narratives found in the books of Exodus, Numbers, Joshua and 1 Samuel. These tell of the Exodus from Egypt, the wanderings of the people in the wilderness and their eventual arrival in the land they had been promised. Despite its length, Psalm 78 does not pretend to be a complete account of this history. Much is omitted, for instance the events at Mount Sinai and the giving of the Ten Commandments. But to recall the prologue, the aim is not to rehearse history for its own sake but to enable the people to *learn* from it. This is what has dictated the psalmist's choice of material.

The psalm cuts to the chase at verse 9, an abrupt indictment of the northern kingdom ('the Ephraimites') for refusing to honour the covenant. 'They forgot' the great works of God, specifically the deliverance from Egypt and the displays of divine power that accompanied it (9–16). And this pattern of unbelief is nothing new. It goes back to the earliest days in the wilderness: 'Yet they sinned still more against him, rebelling against the Most High in the desert' (17), a despondent refrain that occurs three more times in the psalm (32, 40 and 56), each time introducing a new cycle of disobedience. What makes it reprehensible is that it flies in the face of the evidence, plain to see, of God's saving purposes. The episode here is the people's hunger in the desert, and their taunt: ' "Can God spread a table in the wilderness? . . . Can he also give bread, or provide meat for his people?" ' (19–20; see Exodus 16, Numbers 11). God's response was to give them what they craved (21–29), but in outrage at their lack of faith (21–22). The gift was accompanied by a severe judgement: 'the anger of God rose against them and he killed the strongest of them, and laid low the flower of Israel' (31).

The next section (32–37) recalls how the Israelites turned back to God in penitence, but it questions their sincerity: 'they flattered him with their mouths; they lied to him with their tongues' (36). Despite this, God withheld the full expression of his anger, for 'he remembered that they were but flesh, a wind that passes and does not come again', offering instead forgiveness out of compassion for their frailty (38–39). Yet the cycle of rebellion began again (40–41), for once more, they 'did not keep in mind his power' (42). Yet again there is a recital of God's past deeds of deliverance, this time focusing on the plagues of Egypt (43–51), the passage of the Hebrews across the sea to safety (52–53) and their entry into the land (54–55; cf. Exodus 7–15: many decades are compressed into the last few verses of this section).

The final account of rebellion and failure brings events into the community's more recent past, the era of their settlement in the land (56–64). The focus returns to the northern kingdom and its betrayals. '[They] turned away and were faithless like their ancestors; they twisted like a treacherous bow. For they provoked him to anger with their high places; they moved him to jealousy with their idols' (57–58). The condemnation is that they separated themselves from Judah and set up illicit shrines in rivalry to the divinely sanctioned holy place of Zion. So God rejected the northern kingdom of Israel (59), handing over the people to the enemy. This is probably a reference to the deportations that followed the Assyrian invasion of 721 BCE, which resulted in the effective end of the northern kingdom as an entity. After this, only Judah remained. But for the psalmist, her survival with her land, her temple and her monarchy intact is evidence that the divine purpose was focused on her all along. The implication is that she alone has been faithful to YHWH. Loyalty and its rewards is the principal lesson the psalmist wants to draw out of his long and complex narrative.

The high drama of this psalm makes it one of the most colourful in the Psalter. It does, however, raise difficult questions for today's readers, chiefly its portrayal of an angry God who exacts judgement on the unfaithful. This problem is of course already raised by the narratives in the books of Exodus and Numbers themselves. It is not entirely an answer to say that what matters is the psalmist's underlying belief in divine providence and in a morally coherent universe where obedience to God is to reflect the divine ordering of the cosmos, and to disobey him is to violate it, for the language and imagery are still savage even when their intent is recognized. But it does mean that the difficulty is similar to the 'curses' of the laments where we hear the same cry for divine justice to be re-established. We have already met this issue in Psalm 69 and will come back to it again (Psalms 106, 109 and 137).

Meanwhile, it's important to recall the important theme of how compassion and forgiveness are said to lead God to 'restrain' his anger (38). The psalm ends with the beautiful statement that Judah is guided by the 'upright heart' and 'skilful hand' of her Davidic king (72). The Christian reader sees an inevitable 'how much more' at this point of conclusion. For with the thunder and lightning of the psalm behind us, a christological reading celebrates how the heart and hand of Jesus the Son of David guide us out of the tortuous paths of corruption and wickedness into the divinely appointed ways of peace.

16

Justice, mercy and truth

The Sixteenth Evening: Psalms 82, 83, 84, 85

————◆————

This is an evening of varied experiences. Psalms 84 and 85 are both familiar and well loved. Psalm 82 is a great psalm that deserves to be better known. Psalm 83 must be one of the least known psalms of all.

Psalm 82 is a drama set in the divine council or court presided over by God. The idea of a principal deity set over a pantheon of gods is familiar in the ancient Near East. The Hebrew Bible borrows this imagery in, among other places, the story of Micaiah and the prophets (1 Kings 22.19–23) and, famously, in the opening two chapters of the Book of Job where the Satan or 'adversary' accuses Job in the heavenly court room. The theme of the psalm is to 'try' the question, what is needed for a being to qualify as a 'god'? In the polytheistic environment of the ancient world, where Israel's neighbours worshipped many different deities, this was a central issue for the faith of YHWH. How could it establish its claim to truth and to the loyalty of its adherents? Addressing these questions was critical in enabling the faith of Israel to come into its own among world faiths as an unambiguously monotheistic religion.

From the outset, God (*elohim*) is established as the judge of this question. Addressing the gods or heavenly beings (the same word *elohim*) he puts the charge: ' "How long will you judge unjustly and show partiality to the wicked?" ' (1–2). That is to say, the first qualification for being divine is that a god must be morally without blemish, and practise justice. This is precisely what is at issue. The charge must be supported by evidence. This is provided in the succeeding verses: what the gods have failed to do is to deal fairly with the weak and the orphan, the lowly and the destitute, and to defend the powerless against the wicked (3–4). The vulnerable are those known to the Hebrew Bible as the *'awanim*, God's 'poor' to whom the community was to give special protection, as the prophets of Israel never tired of pointing out. But in this the gods have failed miserably. 'They have neither knowledge nor understanding, they walk around in darkness' (5). They are no better than immoveable artefacts that may look the part but can do nothing for those who worship them – indeed, can do nothing at all, a theme that recurs in similar courtroom scenes in the oracles of the prophet we know as Second Isaiah (Isaiah 40–55).

The verdict (6–7) is swift and absolute. 'You are gods', that is, you say you are gods – yet the evidence denies this. So, despite the epithet 'children of the Most High', they are to suffer the fate of mortals (6–7). It is *Götterdämmerung*, the twilight of the gods. And as they are toppled from their gilded pedestals, there is a corresponding exaltation of God who is enthroned as supreme above them all. 'Rise up, O God, judge the earth; for all the nations belong to you!' So the psalm ends where it began, in the heavens where God reigns above the cosmos.

The theme of this magnificent psalm is not that God is more *powerful* than the other deities but that he is more *ethical*. This, all along, has been the basis for the plea of the laments to deliver the poor sufferer from the hands of the cruel oppressor. Psalm 82 is, if we like, an 'inverted lament', seen from God's point of view. It expresses his undying commitment to take the side of those who cry out to him from under the feet of the wicked with their grandiose designs upon the human race. Be they never so strong, the divine verdict upon corrupted power, whatever its source, is always: 'You are gods; nevertheless you shall die like mortals and fall like any prince.'

Psalm 83 is a vehement lament of the community under threat from a hostile axis of nations (5–8 – most of Israel's historic enemies are here). Their ambition is to annihilate Israel, so that it is 'remembered no more' (4). So the people entreat God not to keep silence or hold his peace, for their enemies are his enemies (1–2). What he must do is to act decisively, as in well-remembered victories in the days of the Judges (9–12, see Judges 4–8). He must do this by the 'shock and awe' tactics of fire and storm (13–15) that will demonstrate divine power (echoes here of Psalm 29). But the end is not their destruction for its own sake, despite the prayer that they may perish (17). Rather, it is that God may be seen and known to be God. 'Fill their faces with shame, so that they may seek your name, O Lord . . . Let them know that you alone, whose name is the Lord, are the Most High over all the earth' (16, 18). So this psalm ends precisely where the last one did, with divine order re-established and the sovereignty of yhwh acknowledged – if not yet in fact, then at least in the imaginative anticipation that prayer lends to people of faith.

After the *Stürm und Drang*, we reach a refreshing oasis in *Psalm 84*. It's a song of pilgrimage that, more than any other, radiates the sheer happiness of those going up to Jerusalem for one of the great festivals. 'How lovely is your dwelling-place, O Lord of hosts!' (1). We have already met the same all-consuming love for the sanctuary in Psalms 42 and 43 where the psalmist, unable to worship with the festal throng, experiences an exquisite pain at his enforced separation from the temple. Here, the joy is as intense as the pain was there. 'My soul longs, indeed it faints for the courts of the Lord; my heart and my flesh sing for joy to the living God' (2). If only he could live there for ever, perhaps unnoticed like a bird or with the humblest of duties as a doorkeeper (3, 4, 10).

If those who live in God's house are happy (4), happy too are pilgrims who are journeying there (5). The central section of the psalm imagines pilgrims on their way to Jerusalem, for whom the road to Zion is the road to heaven itself. They are sustained on their journey by the cooling winter rains (6, suggesting that the feast they are going up to celebrate is the autumn festival of Tabernacles) but more importantly, by the prospect of gazing on the God of gods in Zion (7). This at last is the answer to the longing and fretting of the earlier psalm: 'My soul thirsts for God, for the living God: when shall I come and behold the face of God?' (Psalm 42.2). And because God's presence is closely related to the king's role in safeguarding the temple as the heart of national life, the pilgrim's prayer naturally turns first to him as the people's shield and God's anointed (8–9); and from him to the divine 'sun and shield' himself, the everlasting source of all that is good (11). The third appearance of the word 'happy' at the very end (12) reinforces the sense that this is without doubt the most joyful of all the psalms.

Psalm 85 is another community lament. Like Psalm 83, it portrays a nation facing threat, though it is not named. The images and words of harvest (11–12) hint at a failure of the winter rains rather than the aggression of an enemy, but it is not possible to be sure. However, this psalm faces whatever ordeal it is, in a way very different from Psalm 83. In contrast to the violent anger of that psalm, there is a lambent poignancy about this psalm that makes it the gentlest of laments.

It opens unusually, not by stating the people's predicament and pleading to God for help, but by recalling God's deeds in the past. ' LORD, you were favourable to your land; you restored the fortunes of Jacob. You forgave the iniquity of your people; you pardoned all their sin' (1–2). Having laid a foundation by rehearsing the story of God's goodness to the land, the psalm continues by invoking that good past before God and asking him to act consistently with it. The prayer for restoration is followed by a string of plaintive questions, as if appealing to God's better nature. 'Will you be angry with us for ever? Will you prolong your anger to all generations? Will you not revive us again so that your people may rejoice in you?' (5–6). To do these things, urges the psalmist, would be faithful to the covenant traditions of 'steadfast love' (*hesed*). It would be nothing less than the people's salvation (7).

Here is another psalm where God intervenes to answer the psalmist, possibly through the lips of a temple prophet. 'Let me hear what God the LORD will speak, for he will speak peace to his people' (8). *Shalom* means much more than merely the cessation of war or violence. It stands for the fullness of divine blessing poured out on human beings at every level of their life. In that it expresses the movement of divine love and mercy towards the world, it is close to the New Testament word 'grace'. And the truth is that *shalom*, the 'salvation' of the following verse, becomes more and more expansive until everything is embraced by it. Lament has dropped out of view. What is left is the largest possible vision of God's infinite kindness and generosity. 'Mercy and truth are met together: righteousness and peace have kissed each other. Truth shall flourish out of the earth: and righteousness hath looked down from heaven' (10–11, BCP). The psalm, and with it the evening, ends on a note of both hope and contentment, leaving behind the afterglow of some of the most beautiful verses in the Bible.

17

From confidence to despair

The Seventeenth Evening: Psalm 89

———◆———

We are accustomed to the idea that religion should make us feel better about the world and about ourselves. So, traditionally, the 'movement' of faith leads us from darkness into life, from chaos into order, from despair into hope. We have already seen that this is indeed how many of the psalms reflect on life's vicissitudes. To practise lament and name trouble or distress before God is already to have begun the journey that leads, by the end, to a sense of resolution, the 'certainty of a hearing'.

However, a handful of psalms do not make that journey; rather they do it in reverse, drawing the worshipper somewhat disconcertingly not out of the darkness but *into* it. Among them are two neighbours that fall on the Seventeenth Day. The Morning psalms conclude with 88, the most despairing psalm in the book, which ends with a Hebrew word related to darkness. And although Psalm 89 follows it with an opening that is bright with praise and celebration, it is not long before this long and elaborate psalm is plunged into shadow. By the end, the sun has been entirely eclipsed and, apart from the last few words which need careful explanation, the conclusion turns out to be as desperate as its predecessor.

The theme of the psalm is established at once in the opening verses. This song will be about God's covenant love or *hesed* (1), as firm as the heavens themselves (2). The first section of the psalm (5–18) is a celebration of God as the creator who puts the chaotic forces in their place and establishes order in the cosmos, a theme we have already met in Psalm 74. But this is not by itself the psalmist's principal focus. The introduction sets out where the psalm's concerns lie: ' "I have made a covenant with my chosen one, I have sworn to my servant David: 'I will establish your descendants for ever and build your throne for all generations' " ' (3–4). For the psalmist, what demonstrates God's faithfulness more even than the splendour of creation is the historical fact that he has established a kingdom, a people ruled over by David and his descendants to whom specific, inalienable promises have been made.

What these promises consist of is set out in the psalm's central section, 19–37. This key passage, 'royal' in character, is closely related to an episode in the story of David where the young king plans to build a temple to honour YHWH his god. The prophet Nathan tells David that, on the contrary, it is God who is going to build David a 'house', that is, a dynasty that will last for ever. God will be a 'father' to the king, and establish his throne in safety and prosperity. In turn, the king must be faithful to YHWH and loyal to the terms of this covenant. However, even if the king disobeys the covenant and incurs punishment, nevertheless, YHWH will not permanently remove his covenant love from him (2 Samuel 7.5–16). All this is rehearsed in the psalm as it builds up to the climax of this section that takes us back to the stability and trustworthiness of the creation with which the psalm began: ' "Once and for all I have sworn by my holiness; I will not lie to David. His line shall continue for ever, and his throne endure before me like the sun. It shall be established for ever like the moon, an enduring witness in the skies" ' (35–37).

In English, the word 'but' that introduces the next section is tiny enough. In Hebrew, it's no more than the single consonant *waw* attached to the word it qualifies. But one consonant is all it takes to eclipse the light that has so radiantly bathed the psalm up to now. And at once we see the painful issue that has occasioned this psalm. 'But now you have spurned and rejected him . . . You have renounced the covenant with your servant; you have defiled his crown in the dust' (38–39). It is clear that the nation has been overrun by an enemy, the king deposed if not put to death, the kingdom in ruins. 'You have broken through all his walls; you have laid his strongholds in ruins. All who pass by plunder him; he has become the scorn of his neighbours' (40–41). While it is impossible to be certain, the historical event that best fits this outpouring of grief is the Babylonian invasion and conquest of Jerusalem in 587 BCE. This is similar to what we shall see in Psalm 137 ('By the waters of Babylon we sat down and wept') and have already explored in Psalm 74.

In the face of the collapse of everything that made Judah a nation – her monarchy, her temple and, above all, the inviolable covenant of YHWH that imparted her unique identity – the psalm ends with an outpouring of grief-stricken lament as passionate as any in the Psalter: 'How long, O LORD? Will you hide yourself for ever? How long will your wrath burn like fire? . . . Where is your steadfast love of old, which by your faithfulness you swore to David?' (46, 49). It is moving to see how the psalmist, even in despair, goes on appealing to the covenant as the ground of prayer and longing. This is not quite hope. It is, however, to root lament in the historical experience of divine loyalty to his people: if God has proved faithful to his covenant in the past, will he not once again deliver them even at this point of being overwhelmed by alien forces against which no human power can prevail? The key word here is 'remember' (47, 50). It matters that the believer should recall a past in which God himself proved trustworthy. It matters even more that God should recall it, and act.

So the structure of this psalm is now clear: a hymn of praise for creation on which is built a celebration of God's eternal covenant through the king. Because this covenant has now failed, a lament has been added on in such a way as totally to change the nature of what has gone before. There remains the question of the abrupt change of mood in the final verse: 'Blessed be the LORD for ever. Amen and Amen' (52). Is this the psalmist recovering his nerve and finding the hope that has so patently eluded him in the lament that went before? Unfortunately not. The explanation lies simply in the fact that this psalm concludes the third division of the Psalter, and, as we have already seen at the end of Psalm 41, each of the five books of the Psalter ends with an act of praise or doxology (see also Psalm 72.18–20, 106.48, 150). It is true that as an editorial 'marker' of the conclusion to Book III, the doxology has the effect of pulling the reader back into the attitude of praise. As the Orthodox *kontakion* for the departed has it: 'even at the grave we sing alleluia'. But this 'alleluia' is still in a minor key.

The experience of failed promises is one of the bitterest of human experiences. Social scientists speak of 'cognitive dissonance' as a common way of making sense of situations where history has turned out to be different from what was confidently expected or hoped. Perhaps, we tend to say, we did not correctly 'read' events at the time, or maybe what has happened will indeed turn out to be as predicted, even if this cannot be seen for now. What this psalm shows is that we must not flinch from events as they are, however awkwardly they fit with the assumptions we bring to them. The contradiction between covenant promise and historical fact is set out on the Seventeenth Evening in all its bleakness and bewilderment. The psalmist does not attempt to reconcile what the tradition has taught him to believe and what he sees with his own eyes.

Yet the fact that the faith community of the Old Testament not only survived the catastrophic events of the sixth century BCE but flourished in new and undreamed of ways shows that the stark ending of Book III was in no way the end of faith itself. Rather, it is an instance of the biblical pattern of death and life summed up by Jesus in the Fourth Gospel: 'unless a grain of wheat falls into the earth and dies, it remains just a single grain; but if it dies, it bears much fruit' (John 12.24). The exile would prove a long and dark Good Friday. The psalmist could not envisage how any dawn could follow it. But the perspective of resurrection faith casts a new radiance on this dark night of Israel's soul. In the depths of his lament, the psalmist asks the question we have already faced in Psalm 49: 'Who can live and never see death? Who can escape the power of Sheol?' (48). The psalmist's implied answer is one thing. The answer of Easter Day is quite another.

18

Judge eternal throned in splendour
The Eighteenth Evening: Psalms 93, 94

The Eighteenth and Nineteenth Evenings begin in the same way, with a ringing acclamation of YHWH the divine king, enthroned in majesty above the world he has made. In one sense, every evening begins and ends here, for every psalm is in one way or another an acknowledgement of God's reign, and the offering of an aspect of human life in the light of his sovereignty; this is what religious faith is. If it were any different, there would be no point in offering either praise or lament because there would be no point in believing.

However, there is an important group of psalms whose specific theme is the kingship of God. These are known as *enthronement psalms*. We have already met one at Psalm 47, 'O clap your hands all you peoples'. *Psalm 93* introduces a cluster of enthronement psalms that includes 96–99. These have in common the cry 'YHWH is king!' (or similar words) which, in tonight's psalm and in 97 and 99, form the opening words. Some scholars dispute whether the usual translation, 'The LORD *is* king' is correct. They would prefer 'The LORD *has become* king' (for the Hebrew verb is indeed in the perfect tense). This is because, as we saw in Psalm 47, the enthronement psalms may have originated in a temple 'enthronement' ceremony in which the ritual abasement and exaltation of the (human) king was thought to actualize God's own kingship over the people and guarantee the benefits this brought to the land: victory over enemies and the fertility of the crops. So the shout 'The LORD has become king!' would mark the culmination of the ritual, and affirm that divine order had been restored in the face of the ever-present threat of chaos.

There may well be truth in these much-argued theories, though direct evidence is patchy. However, the perfect tense inevitably carries a present implication. If God 'has become' king, then this is what he now is, and this is what Psalm 93 celebrates in exultant tones.

Psalm 93 is the purest example of an enthronement psalm. The opening acclamation of YHWH as king is given vivid colour by imagining him as 'robed' in splendour. We shall meet this image again in another psalm, where God is 'clothed with honour and majesty, wrapped in light as with a garment' (104.1–2). But this is no empty claim, as the heart of this short psalm makes clear. God demonstrates his kingship by creating the world as an immoveable, solid, trustworthy place. 'He has established the world; it shall never be moved' (1). This is in absolute contrast to the turbulent, chaotic waters the psalmist goes on to describe. The threefold repetition of 'floods' in verse 3 hints at the desperate anxiety the threat of the unrestrained waters held for an ancient society. But though wave and water thunder terrifyingly, there is One who is above them. The threefold floods are answered by a threefold majesty (4): 'more majestic than the thunders of mighty waters, more majestic than the waves of the sea, majestic on high is the LORD!' The psalm ends on a note of stability: not only is the creation reliably firm, but so are the decrees that made it so (5), by which the cosmos, the community of the covenant, the house of God and its worshippers are all governed.

This watery imagery is everywhere in the Psalter. We have seen it in the lament of the sufferer for whom it is as if the waters have come up to his neck (69.1) and in the hymn of praise to the LORD who 'gathered the waters of the sea as in a bottle; he put the deeps in storehouses' (33.7). These all echo the creation story of Genesis where, in the beginning, the universe was a 'formless void'. Over this chaotic primordial 'deep' the wind or Spirit of God swept (Genesis 1.1–2) so as to bring pattern and life to birth. The emergence of order is the result of a series of acts of divine 'separation': light from darkness, waters from sky, waters from dry land. The emergence of order out of chaos is the fundamental theme in the creation myths of all ancient societies. In the 'Babylonian Creation Epic' the god joins battle with the monster of the deep and overcomes her, after which dry land and life appear. We saw in an earlier psalm how this imagery of the primeval battle was pressed into service to bolster faith in a God who was greater than the chaos that had overwhelmed the people (74.12–17).

It would be difficult to overestimate the importance of this theme in the Psalter. The vast majority of Psalms belong to the 'life setting' of temple worship, as we have frequently noticed. In a precarious and unstable world, religion was the prime means of establishing a sense of confidence and security under the protection of the deity. It offered a defence against the many ways in which an ever-present chaos, lurking around the edges of civilization, threatened to overwhelm an ancient society, whether through natural disaster or human agency. Faith did this by creating its own ordered universe as a bulwark against chaos: the architecture of the temple itself, the rituals of its worship, and the moral and ethical laws by which a community lived. Today, this aspect of religious faith is perhaps disparaged in the West, because it seems to imply an immature kind of dependence. However, faith is always about acknowledging dependence and recognizing that without God, human life is empty and chaotic.

This is where faith 'adds value'. It offers a larger context within which to live and flourish. It's futile to think that the threats of chaos are any less today than they were in the ancient world; indeed, they are more terrifying because they are not simply personal or local but are now global in extent: climate change, economic meltdown, war and terrorism, hunger and disease. In the face of a world as uncertain as ours, the enthronement psalms offer a bigger vision of things. It may feel as though it is crying in the wind to repeat 'more majestic . . . more majestic . . . majestic on high'. But the last verse of the psalm provides both the key to understanding it, and the mandate for living it out. 'Holiness befits your house' (5) – the holiness not only of the Almighty himself, but of those who frequent the temple, and who in doing so commit themselves to live in the light of God's decrees for the good ordering of human life and society and of the planet itself.

The second psalm is a dark and passionate lament. After the heights scaled by its predecessor, we might think that *Psalm 94* would drag the evening down. But that would be to misunderstand Psalm 93. For the kingship of God was demonstrated precisely by his sovereignty over the *depths*. This psalm offers us a specific instance of how the worshipper responds to the threat of chaos in history; in this case, the invasion of an enemy. The message is the same, for the psalmist begins by invoking 'the judge of the earth' (2) to whom vengeance belongs (1), and ends with the familiar and reassuring thought that God is his 'stronghold' and his 'rock' (22). This is still the 'majestic' God of Psalm 93 whose decrees are 'very sure'.

The psalm begins as a community lament bemoaning the onslaught of the foe, particularly the enemy's treatment of the poor and voiceless (2–6). We have met their taunts before: ' "The LORD does not see; the God of Jacob does not perceive" ' (7). Here, their scorn is cleverly answered by a series of rhetorical questions addressed to the fools (those who say in their hearts, 'there is no God', 53.1). 'He who planted the ear, does he not hear? He who formed the eye, does he not see?' (8–11). In other words, far from being distant, YHWH is ever present to his people (12–14) to lead and guide them into the paths of safety and wisdom. Here the community recedes from the psalmist's thoughts, and his individual condition comes to the fore, for the rest of the psalm is in 'I' form. Despite the conspiracies of the wicked, God remains his strength and will both deliver him from the enemy's power and exact vengeance where it is due.

So the psalm comes full circle, as very often in the Psalter. 'Vengeance', as we have seen, means God's intention to re-establish the world as a just and ethical place. And this entails dealing with all that disorders the universe and usurps the goodness and justice of his reign. In the previous psalm, it was the watery flood. Here it is the enemy. The truth is the same, and it calls for the same faith – often, it has to be said, against all the odds – in the God of Israel who is both our Creator and Deliverer.

19

The divine and human king

The Nineteenth Evening:
Psalms 98, 99, 100, 101

———◆◆◆———

The first three psalms this evening are nothing less than worldwide in scope. The enthronement Psalms 98 and 99 acclaim YHWH as king not only over Israel but over all the nations on earth. Psalm 100 invites the whole world to come into his presence and worship him for his faithfulness and love. Music and song pervade these well-known hymns of praise. But then the less familiar Psalm 101 strikes a more sober note as if to remind us that to sing and play to the glory of God always has ethical consequences.

Psalm 98 exalts YHWH as the triumphant King. *Cantate Domino*: 'O sing to the LORD a new song, for he has done marvellous things.' What precisely this victory is not directly stated. But the imagery of God's 'right hand and his holy arm' (1) is virtually a direct quotation from the song of Moses following the Hebrews' triumphant Exodus from Egypt (Exodus 15.6, 12, 16). We can safely say that this psalm is a celebration of God's mighty acts of deliverance, of which Israel's passing through the Red Sea was the paradigm. And this is nothing less than God's 'remembering' his promises of old to his people whereby he pledged himself to them in 'steadfast love and faithfulness' (3), or perhaps we could better say, in 'loyal covenant love'.

So, the remainder of the psalm is a summons to worship this God of victories. The 'joyful noise' is the music of temple worship, of course, both choral and instrumental (5–6). We have seen more than once how the language of psalms such as these is liturgical through and through. But the singing and dancing are not restricted to the sanctuary; indeed it is impossible that they could be contained there. The invitation to worship is addressed to 'all the earth' (4). This is where the psalm reaches its climax, with the whole of creation leading the song of victory, its inarticulate sounds speaking beyond themselves to join in the hymn of the universe to its Creator.

There is one further theme here that connects this psalm to Psalm 94, where the previous evening ended. There, the psalmist cried to YHWH to 'rise up' and vindicate himself before the world's peoples. This is precisely what tonight's Psalm 98 says he has done: 'The LORD has made known his victory; he has revealed his vindication in the sight of the nations' (2). Once again, Egypt is the paradigm: what God did at the exodus he can do again. So the psalm ends with a final reason for singing the 'new song' to God: for 'he is coming to judge the earth. He will judge the world with righteousness, and the peoples with equity' (9). His victory is more than a display of naked power. It is the victory of justice, the right ordering of the world and of human life that is at the heart of ethical faith. The world has nothing to fear from such a God.

The next psalm is in the same vein. *Psalm 99* begins with a vision of the LORD as the exalted King, 'enthroned upon the cherubim', that is, in the supreme place of glory. What else can the earth and its peoples do but tremble with reverence and awe (1)? Again, 'all the peoples' are summoned to worship. And, touchingly, the psalmist includes himself in this universal act of praise. For here the third person 'he' that has featured in all of Psalms 96 to 99 suddenly turns into the direct second person 'you', as the psalmist comes to address God himself. 'Let them praise your great and awesome name. Holy is he!' (3). The refrain 'Holy is he!' recurs twice more (5, 9), an echo of how an earlier enthronement psalm ended: 'holiness befits your house, O LORD' (Psalm 93.5). Perhaps Psalm 99 can be seen as a poetic commentary on Isaiah's great temple vision where at the outset of his ministry the prophet gazes upon the glory of God and hears the song of the angels, ' "Holy, holy, holy is the LORD of hosts" ' (Isaiah 6.3).

Like Psalm 98, this psalm sees God's victory as the establishment of justice (4). It invokes three key characters from the history of Israel as examples: Moses and Aaron from the Exodus and wilderness period, and Samuel from the time the monarchy was inaugurated (6–8). The emphasis is on how they 'called on his name . . . and he answered them'. So once again, God's victory is not seen as a matter of coercion but the outcome of a relationship: 'they called . . . they cried . . . he answered . . . they kept his decrees . . . you were a forgiving God to them'. But there is a final attribute in the series. The psalmist has not forgotten that Israel's career since the beginning had been wayward and fickle: 'you were . . . an avenger of their wrongdoings' (8). There is always a costly aspect to the victory that is premised, not on the assumption often made by religious people that 'my God is stronger than yours', but on the claim upon us of the moral and ethical requirements of our faith.

Psalm 100 is the familiar *Jubilate Deo*, best known to English-speakers through its metrical version 'All people that on earth do dwell'. This Morning canticle in the BCP service of Matins (where it is an alternative to the *Benedictus*) has strayed into Cranmer's Evening psalm cycle. But morning or evening, the summons to worship God is addressed to 'all the earth', and in this respect, this little psalm is an apt response to the exultant enthronement psalms that precede it. Once again temple worship is to the fore: 'come into his presence' (2), 'enter his gates with thanksgiving, and his courts with praise (4). There is to be music and song. Why? Because YHWH is our Creator and King (we recall from Psalm 23 that the 'shepherd–sheep' image refers directly to kingship). More than this, for a Creator–King might not necessarily be *kind* as well as mighty, he is 'good', his *hesed* or 'steadfast love' will never fail, and his faithfulness will last for ever.

After all this *forte* and *fortissimo*, the final psalm of the evening, *Psalm 101*, is *mezzo-piano* at most. It begins music-ally, in tune with all three previous psalms: 'I will sing . . .' (1). His song, says the psalmist, will be of 'loyalty and justice' – themes that we have seen are very much present in the enthronement psalms. But whereas there, the tone was public and extraverted, here it is much more inward in character: 'I will study the way that is blameless. When shall I attain it?' (2).

It isn't immediately obvious who this 'I' is. Clearly, it's someone who is possessed – some might say obsessed – with what Psalm 69 called 'zeal' for God's house. The psalm is a string of resolutions introduced by the promise: 'I will walk with integrity of heart within my house'. Most of these are negative. The psalmist will not tolerate anything base (3), disloyal (4) or perverse (5). He will bring retribution upon the slanderer and the proud (5). But while he will honour the faithful and pious (6), the deceitful will be cast out (7) and all the wicked be destroyed, 'cutting off all evildoers from the city of the LORD' (8).

This could all be read as an unpleasantly self-righteous catalogue of the psalmist's virtues in contrast with the vices of the wicked. It would be like the Pharisee praying in the temple, 'God, I thank you that I am not like other people: thieves, rogues, adulterers, or even like this tax-collector' (Luke 18.11). But there is one person who could speak in this way, perhaps: not an ordinary worshipper, but one who had been given the guardianship of the temple, the protector of its sanctity as a place of truth and justice. The obvious candidate for this role is the Israelite king, for whom in a precise technical sense, the temple was indeed his specific responsibility, and could therefore accurately be described as 'my house' (2, 7). Indeed, the king wants the ethical purity of the temple to be a symbol of a kingdom purged of evil (8). So the psalm is best seen as the lament of a righteous king bemoaning the presence of evil in the kingdom, but pledging himself to uphold 'the way that is blameless' (2), which is the way of God's covenant and teaching.

We have seen in the enthronement psalms how victory is pre-eminently an issue of truth and justice, not of power. Perhaps this psalm is the Nineteenth Evening's 'conscience'. It's the best possible antidote to the kind of triumphalism that could sing Psalms 98–100 without asking the more searching questions about what God's righteous demands on us are. The answer is that to 'enter his gates with thanksgiving, and his courts with praise' (100.4) means taking upon ourselves what God requires of his faithful people, as the prophet puts it, 'to do justly, to love mercy and to walk humbly with the LORD our God' (Micah 6.8). We can make the 'I' of the psalm our resolve, not in any self-aggrandizing way (as if we were kings ourselves!) but by humbly submitting ourselves to the way of God. Perhaps the true speaker in this psalm is Christ himself, King and Servant of all, in whose life we see that divine pattern of holiness lived out to perfection, and in whose death and resurrection the way of truth is opened up for all to embrace with joy.

20

Pavilioned in splendour

The Twentieth Evening: Psalm 104

———•◆•———

The Twentieth Evening is one of the jewels of the Psalter, an immaculately crafted song in praise of creation. It is the basis of one of the best hymns in the English language, Robert Grant's 'O worship the King all glorious above', superbly married to William Croft's fine tune *Hanover*. To us, the beauty of this incomparable poem reflects the beauty of the natural world it describes. To those who once sang this song during the temple cult, it was much more a celebration of the harvest and a thanksgiving to the God who had once again blessed the people through the gift of a fruitful land.

The psalms of creation form an important group in the Psalter, as we have already seen in Psalms 8 and 33 (to which we should add the morning Psalms 19 and 139). There are important connections, too, with the enthronement psalms that recall God's victory of the primeval chaos. But *Psalm 104* is by far the longest and most elaborate treatment of creation in the Psalter. It is the Psalter's poetic commentary on the creation narratives in the Book of Genesis. More surprisingly, this psalm turns out to have indisputable links with the (older) Egyptian Hymn to Aten the sun disk, from which it derives a large number of its key words and images. Scholars have speculated about how this might have come about. The cult of Aten belonged to the extraordinary 'Amarna' era of the fourteenth century BCE when, for reasons that are not clear, Egyptian religion abandoned its polytheism and under the Pharaoh Akhenaten embraced monotheism for a while through the cult of Aten. It is conjectured that Psalm 104 might have begun life as an Egyptian hymn to the sun that was largely 'transferred' to the worship of Israel's God YHWH. (We saw that in much the same way, Psalm 29 may once have been a hymn to the Canaanite storm-god Baal that was pressed into service as a hymn in praise of YHWH.)

What we do know is that in the civilizations of the ancient Near East such as Egypt and Babylon, circles of the 'wise' enjoyed a good deal of cultural and intellectual exchange. Israel also belonged to this cosmopolitan world, and this psalm is not the only text in the Hebrew Bible to show clear influences from outside the borders of Israelite society. This is a striking insight into the presence of the 'divine' in human thought and art. To the author of this psalm, the God of the covenant is committed to the whole of his creation, not simply to Israel. 'Monotheism' entails the claim that the entire cosmos owes allegiance to the true God who has manifested his power and his goodness in fashioning creation. Whatever the origins of this psalm, there is no disputing that this is the psalmist's conviction. In our contemporary world, Psalm 104 inspires a mature theology of 'common grace' in which, recognized or not, the Spirit of God is at work in all the intricate processes of creation (30), as well as in the activity of human beings in every aspect of civilization where divine creativity and wise governance are reflected.

The psalm falls into three clear sections. It begins (1–9) by painting on the grandest of canvasses. The magnificent project of creation is set out in noble poetry only equalled in the Bible by the incomparable opening chapter of Genesis and the great 'creation' passages of Job 38 and 39. Who is YHWH whom the psalmist begins by blessing? Nothing less than the God of the universe who is 'very great' (1), 'clothed with honour and majesty, wrapped in light as with a garment'. The vastness of the cosmos is the demonstration of both his power and his artistry: the vault of the heavens, the towering clouds and terrifying storm winds are all subject to him (2–4). So, too, are the primeval waters, in ancient mythology representing the threat of disorder, as we have already seen in the enthronement psalms. In this psalm, the earth's stability, 'set on its foundations so that it shall never be shaken' (5), is testimony to the God who establishes inviolable boundaries that define the dry land and keep the chaotic waters in their place, never again to threaten God's world (7–9).

Where the opening section paints with the broadest possible brush, the middle section lovingly fills in the intimate detail (10–23). Its focus is the infinite variety of life with which the earth teems, thanks to the goodness of the Creator. The link with the first section is water. But now the springs and streams are stripped of the mythological power the waters had when God subdued them at the beginning of time. Here, they exist simply to give birth to and nourish life, 'giving drink to every wild animal; the wild asses quench their thirst. By the streams the birds of the air have their habitation; they sing among the branches' (10–12). All this is God's gift: 'from your lofty abode you water the mountains; the earth is satisfied with the fruit of your work' (13). Later on, water is for life-bearing, transport and recreation (the once terrifying sea-monster, stripped of his mythological power, now simply *plays*): 'Yonder is the sea, great and wide, creeping things innumerable are there, living things both small and great. There go the ships, and Leviathan that you formed to sport in it' (25–26).

From this flows all the fruitfulness that makes for the earth's flourishing and the sustaining of human life: grass for the cattle, plants for cultivation, the benefits that follow in the necessary staples of wine, oil and bread. Not only this, the natural world has its own self-sustaining cycles of life: the trees where birds nest, and the mountains and rocks where wild creatures wander at will (14–18). And this bewildering array of life is given shape by the daily cycle of light and darkness, defining the rhythms that mark the lives of human beings no less than of the other creatures with which we share the planet: 'The young lions roar for their prey, seeking their food from God. When the sun rises, they withdraw and lie down in their dens. People go out to their work and to their labour until the evening' (21–23).

We sense that the psalmist could go on and on filling in this depiction of a world that to him glows with the goodness and care of its Creator. His sense of the goodness of things recalls the harvest psalms 65 and 67, and it is likely that this psalm belongs to the ceremonies of the autumn when YHWH was blessed for the annual gift of the winter rains fertilizing the earth for another year. In the light of his survey, the psalmist can only return to his opening theme and exclaim with delight and praise how God is the source of all that is good in creation. 'O LORD, how manifold are your works! In wisdom you have made them all; the earth is full of your creatures' (24). This final section (24–35) gathers up themes from earlier in the psalm, particularly the dependence of all living things on their Creator: 'These all look to you to give them their food in due season; when you give it to them, they gather it up; when you open your hand, they are filled with good things' (27–28).

What is new in this last part of Psalm 104 is an undertow of anxiety that begins to gnaw away at the tone of celebration and joy. God might hide his face and withdraw his life-giving favour: 'when you take away their breath, they die and return to their dust' (29). This, of course, simply serves to underline the theme of creation's dependence on its God: 'When you send forth your spirit, they are created; and you renew the face of the ground' (30). But fear is not entirely allayed; after all, the God of all living things has already been worshipped as the fiery God of the storm-wind. So the psalmist's conclusion is filled with a proper sense of reverence, lest the intimate beauty of the world mislead anyone as to the awesome, untameable power of its Maker. 'May the glory of the LORD endure for ever; may the LORD rejoice in his works – who looks on the earth and it trembles, who touches the mountains and they smoke' (31–32).

In a brief coda, the psalmist vows to make the worship of God his lifelong theme: 'I will sing to the LORD as long as I live; I will sing praise to my God while I have being' (33). Yet here, he suddenly sounds a warning note. 'Let sinners be consumed from the earth, and let the wicked be no more' (35). Perhaps this feels intrusive and jarring to our modern ears, not attuned to the abrupt ways in which semitic poetry can range across the extremes of human experience. The imprecation, as we have seen from the laments, is not so much a curse on the wicked as a prayer for divine order to be established on the earth. As the psalmist's penultimate word, there is an aptness about it. From his vantage point, it seems as though the only risk to the beauty and order of the world is humankind's occupancy of it. So, his prayer that human society may be as well ordered and patterned as the created order is both natural and right. And it prevents the psalm from collapsing into a romantic nature-poem as if it could somehow be blissfully ignorant of what spoils and corrupts the earth. The final blessing, indeed, celebrates creation as the wonderful entity it already is, but also anticipates a more glorious future when the goals intended for it by its Maker are reached. The 'now' is 'very good', as God said when he finished his work of creation (Genesis 1.28). The 'not yet' which the psalm looks forward to will be even better.

This psalm speaks directly into our twenty-first-century concerns about the environment and the future of our planet. Its prayer that sinners may be destroyed can perhaps be read as longing for the time when the earth will be free of all that exploits it, irreparably damaging its wonderful yet delicate fabric and posing real risks to life and civilization as we know it. The threats of chaos, so much feared by the Hebrews, are alive in our own day in innumerable and frightening forms, and we are right to fear them too. If sheer love of creation does not drive us as a race and as individual people to do our utmost to save the global environment, perhaps fear can and should. That such a cherished psalm in praise of the beauty of creation should end on a note of trepidation should make us all stop and think about our own part in the life and welfare of this good earth.

21

Lest we forget

The Twenty-first Evening: Psalm 106

The previous evening, the Twentieth, ushered in a fine sequence of long psalms, each of which has a morning or an evening to itself in the Prayer Book cycle. Psalm 104 is a glowing hymn celebrating the acts of God in creation. Psalm 105 continues the theme of telling the story of God's 'wonderful works' (105.2) by recalling how the Hebrews were (in the literal sense of the word) 'wonderfully' delivered from Egypt, kept safe through the years of wilderness wandering and finally installed in their own land. Between them, these two psalms encapsulate the heart of Israel's *kerygma*, her faith in a covenant God who had both created the world and redeemed Israel as his chosen people.

Psalm 106 tells the same story as 105, but from a quite different perspective. Its first few verses are deceptive. The invitation to 'praise the LORD! O give thanks to the LORD, for he is good; for his steadfast love endures for ever' (1) is very similar to the start of 105 and virtually identical to the opening of another great hymn of praise, Psalm 136. We imagine that this joyful note of celebration will be continued through 106 as well. But it is not to be. In the prayer that follows there are already hints of a minor key: 'Remember me, O LORD, when you show favour to your people; help me when you deliver them' (4–5). The sun may have risen in a clear sky, but it is not long before clouds begin to obscure it.

The hues become rapidly more sombre. 'Both we and our ancestors have sinned; we have committed iniquity, we have done wickedly' (6). This is not simply some general acknowledgement of human frailty but the psalmist's recognition of a specific strain of rebelliousness on the part of the people. What made their unbelief particularly culpable was that it went right back to the founding events of their story, and this in the face of the demonstrable evidence of all that God was doing for his people. 'Our ancestors, when they were in Egypt, did not consider your wonderful works; they did not remember the abundance of your steadfast love, but rebelled against the Most High at the Red Sea' (7). And this becomes the depressing theme of this long recital of Israel's waywardness. She had been redeemed from slavery, and set on the long march to freedom. Yet inwardly there was no redemption and, therefore, no true liberation. The message of the psalm is that this people were as enslaved as ever in their hearts. Freedom for the psalmist still lies in the future. In his carefully crafted confession he is careful to link past and present, and personally to acknowledge his own part in the people's rebellion: 'Both we and our ancestors have sinned' (6).

Like Psalm 78 with which this psalm has much in common, God constantly acts in spite of the people's unbelief and ingratitude. 'Yet he saved them for his name's sake, so that he might make known his mighty power' (8). Faced with the signs and wonders of the Exodus, there is, to be sure, a period of obedience: 'Then they believed his words; they sang his praise' (12). However, it doesn't last long: 'But they soon forgot his works' (13). Forgetfulness is the fundamental issue of this psalm (see 21), for which the people are both culpable and to be pitied. To the psalmist this spiritual amnesia is not only unforgivable but incomprehensible: contrast how God himself does not forget but 'remembers' his covenant (45).

This interplay of divine memory and human forgetting follows the way the stories are told in the books of Exodus and Numbers. The central section (13–33) is an indictment of the Hebrews for their failure of memory and their lack of faith in the desert. A long catena of episodes reinforces this bleak message. No sooner have they crossed the sea than they 'test' God by demanding to be fed (14–15, cf. Exodus 16–17). Then envy sets in, represented by the rebellion of Dathan and Abiram (16–18, see Numbers 16) whose grumbling against Moses led to a spectacular display of judgement. Next comes the episode of the golden calf (19–23, cf. Exodus 32) made by Aaron at the insistence of the people, an act in defiance not only of Moses' leadership but of the covenant itself. All this was tantamount to 'despising' what was promised (24) while they 'grumbled in their tents and did not obey the voice of the LORD' (25).

There is, however, always a divine 'yet', which is God's refusal to treat the people as contemptuously as they have treated him. Just as he saved them from the enemy despite their rebellion (8), so twice he restrains himself from executing the judgement that their behaviour merits. On both occasions, this is at the behest of a human intercessor. The first time it is Moses who, after the incident of the golden calf, stays God's act of execution. 'Therefore he said he would destroy them – had not Moses, his chosen one, stood in the breach' (23). The prayer attributed to Moses (Exodus 32.1–14) movingly asks God to 'remember' his promises of old, and not to bring himself into disrepute by appearing to be fickle in his treatment of the Hebrews. The second occasion (24–31) occurred when the Hebrews had fallen into idolatry (the worship of 'Baal of Peor') and engaged in illicit sexual activity with non-Israelites (Numbers 24.1–13). In the ensuing plague, thousands of Hebrews perished. However, Phinehas, a grandson of Aaron, demonstrated such zeal for YHWH in acting against one of the transgressors that he was forever remembered as God's favoured priest: 'And that has been reckoned to him as righteousness from generation to generation for ever' (31).

The reader would like the desert to be simply an episode. It would be understandable if straitened circumstances did not bring out the best in the people; but surely they would prove faithful in the environment of a generous and fertile land. However, the final part of the history (34–45) relentlessly drives home the lesson that nothing changed when they entered Canaan. When they should have purified the land of its paganism, the Israelites instead merely made its religious practices their own (34–39). Its depravity is symbolized by the practice of child-sacrifice (37–38), always in the Bible a mark of people who have sold out to the most corrupting behaviour imaginable. In this way, says the psalmist, they not only pollute the land, which is bad enough for it is God's gift; worse, they pollute themselves (38–39) in acts of apostasy that the psalmists, in common with prophets like Hosea, unsparingly call acts of shameless 'prostitution'.

This is why Israel finds herself in her current predicament. Up to now, the psalmist has not mentioned the historical situation in which Israel finds herself. But at the psalm's climax it becomes clear what this long recital is *for*. It is to assert that in a decisive act of history, God has finally done what he had intended to do all along: punish the people for their unfaithfulness. His prayer makes it clear what this refers to: 'Save us, O LORD our God, and gather us from among the nations' (47). The people are overrun and in exile. And this time there is no one to intercede for them. They are on their own before God. 'Then the anger of the LORD was kindled against his people . . . he gave them into the hand of the nations, so that those who hated them ruled over them' (40–41). We are in the sixth century BCE, when Israel is in the alien land of Babylon and crying out in despair, 'How shall we sing the LORD's song in a strange land?' (Psalm 137.4, BCP).

Bleak though this landscape is, the psalmist is not without hope. In a final act of remembering, he recalls how YHWH heard his people when they were oppressed, and saved them (43–46). The cry for deliverance with which the psalm ends is almost no more than a simple coda. But how much poignancy and pain is compressed into the single verse in which the psalmist, taking up the mantle of Moses and Phinheas on behalf of the people, beseeches the LORD to save his people (47). There is no pretence that the story is other than it is, no pitiful excuses or whining self-justification. There is simply the hope, reminiscent of Moses' prayer, that a restored and grateful people will demonstrate God's faithfulness to the world: 'gather us from among the nations, that we may give thanks to your holy name and glory in your praise'. The final verse, a doxology of praise to mark the end of Book IV of the Psalter, also stands as the anticipated thanksgiving of a restored people who can once again say 'amen' to a final act of deliverance.

This catalogue of perversity and its punishment does not exactly lift the spirits. But it reminds us of what we have already seen in Psalm 78, that the lessons of personal and public history are not always comfortable. This psalm is the 'shadow' of its joyful predecessor, Psalm 105. Sometimes we need to tell our story in order to celebrate it, while at other times we need to tell the same story as an act of contrition and lament. Psalm 106 faces up to the propensity of human beings to deceive themselves as to their true state before God and one another. It warns us that self-deceit inevitably leads to downfall, for what we truly are as communities or as individuals will always become plain to see in time. This portrait of a people in rebellion, degraded and debased by their cravings and unable to look beyond them, is scarcely attractive. Yet if the opening chapters of the Letter to the Romans are to be believed (a passage that echoes words and images from this psalm), it is precisely our own predicament that the psalm describes. Its motto could be: 'all have sinned and fallen short of the glory of God' (Romans 3.23).

Yet the covenant has not failed. God's wish and purpose is to heal his broken humanity. The Christian sees in those like Moses, Phinehas and the psalmist himself who 'stand in the breach', pictures of the One who has reconciled us to God and intercedes for humanity before his Father. The prodigal can return home. At the end of this psalm's long and gloomy day, the sun comes out once more.

22

A curse on the enemy

The Twenty-second Evening: Psalms 108, 109

—•◆•—

The notorious Twenty-second Evening includes the most violent psalm in the book. No less than one third of the entire psalmody set for this evening consists of impassioned curse and imprecation (Psalm 109.6–19). It is the Psalter's darkest hour. It raises sharp questions both about what the psalmist himself believed about prayer, and about how a psalm like this could be used (or indeed could be usable) as part of our own spirituality as contemporary men and women.

As a prologue to the evening, *Psalm 108* strikes a defiant note in the face of the enemy. It consists of two sections lifted verbatim from earlier psalms. The first (1–5) is taken from Psalm 57.7–11. That psalm began as a personal lament that dissolved into a song of victory in praise of the God who delivers his people. The triumphant conclusion is what is quoted here. The verbs of celebration are piled up: 'I will sing'; 'I will make melody'; I will give thanks'; 'I will sing praises'. We imagine the psalmist entering the sanctuary to offer a morning sacrifice of thanksgiving: 'Awake, O harp and lyre! I will awake the dawn' (2). His confidence that God will deliver him from his adversaries is based on the covenant (or steadfast) love (*hesed*) that is 'higher than the heavens' (4), the very skies above which in Hebrew imagination God himself is enthroned as sovereign (5).

The second part of the psalm is the same as Psalm 60.5–12, a text we have already met on the Eleventh Evening. Its conclusion, 'it is he who will tread down our foes' (13), provides an apt lead-in to the psalm that follows, for the foe is precisely the focus of that lament. *Psalm 109* is overwhelmed with an ominous sense of dread in the face of the enemy whose omnipresence permeates this terrible song. It is close in spirit to Psalm 69, and some of the points made in our discussion of the Thirteenth Evening will apply here too.

The psalmist's predicament, not for the first time in the Psalter, is that he finds himself besieged by false accusers, again a possible background of Psalm 69. The opening complaint (1–5) emphasizes the destructive power of words when they are used maliciously. 'Wicked and deceitful mouths are opened against me, speaking against me with lying tongues. They beset me with words of hate, and attack me without cause' (2–3). Perhaps he is the victim of false witnesses in the court of law: the frequent juridical language of accusation, trial and condemnation throughout this psalm suggests that this is a very likely setting. If so, that makes it all the worse, for a court is where the complainant has every right to expect words of justice, not vindictive spite. So, amid the onslaught of words intended to maim and destroy, all the more poignant is the opening petition, 'Do not be silent' (1). For if the 'God of my praise' holds his tongue, who will speak up for the innocent?

The heart of Psalm 109 is the curse or imprecation (6–19), a violent upsurge of harsh invective whose fallout we have already felt in the psalm's opening account of the adversary's behaviour towards the psalmist and whose consequences rumble on right to the end. And here we must, for once, take issue with the New Revised Standard Version of the Psalms. Perhaps this passage was too strong for the

130

translators, for they insert without any warrant in the Hebrew text the introductory words 'they say' before launching into this difficult passage which they place entirely within quotation marks. This is meant to transfer all that follows to the lips of the false accuser, as if the psalmist were quoting a curse hurled at *him*. The truth, however hard it is to take, is that it is the opposite way round. These are the words of the desperate sufferer as he pours out his lament to his God in a torrent of rage and bitterness. These are the words of *piety*.

Since there is no way round this passage, we must travel through it. The content is tough, to say the least. It begins with the prayer that the false accuser may know what it is like to be put in the assize as the psalmist is: 'Appoint a wicked man against him . . . when he is tried, let him be found guilty' (6–7). Then follows the punishment the psalmist wishes on him. He will enjoy a brief life (8), his widow and their children will be left penniless and without pity (9–12), they will ultimately be cut off without being memorialized (13), except for the memory of his own shame and that of his forebears (14–15), perpetuated for ever as a sign of the judgement the wicked bring down upon themselves.

At the end of all this, the psalmist lays bare the spiritual logic that leads to his verdict on the oppressor. Here the psalm achieves true depths of tragic poignancy. 'He did not remember to show kindness, but pursued the poor and needy and the broken-hearted to their death. He loved to curse; let curses come on him. He did not like blessing; may it be far from him' (16–17). With acute insight, the psalmist recognizes that the enemy's behaviour has become a habit that is ingrained. It is too late to shed, for it clings to him like clothes steeped in acid; it seeps into his being like a poison. 'He clothed himself with cursing as his coat, may it soak into his body like water, like oil into his bones. May it be like a garment that he wraps around himself, like a belt that he wears every day' (18–19) – just like the proud and violent in Psalm 73.6–9.

It does not seem possible that this psalm could turn itself round from such a dark place. Yet late in the day comes a moment of transformation. 'But you, YHWH my LORD, act on my behalf for your name's sake; because your steadfast love is good, deliver me' (21). The psalmist remembers that the poor are under God's special protection (22–25) and because of this he calls on God to deliver him. For YHWH's treatment of him will be the polar opposite of his accuser's. 'Let them curse, but you will bless' (28). And when God breaks his silence by uttering words of deliverance, the psalmist for his part will open his mouth in praise and thanksgiving (30) – for it is YHWH who is not only his advocate and judge but also his deliverer (31).

What do we make of this psalm? Probably it arouses a double response in us. On the one hand we would be inhuman not to feel compassion for a sufferer so tormented and abused. On the other, that same compassion for our fellow human beings puts a big question mark by the violence of his language against the enemy. We have already touched on this in the context of Psalm 69, but we need to say a little more about it here.

The imprecations of both psalms are referred in the New Testament to the career of Judas Iscariot as the accursed betrayer of Jesus (see Acts 1.20). One way of reading the 'curses' of these psalms is to apply them to those people (or the systems they serve) who manifestly violate the norms of fairness (in the *Divine Comedy* of Dante, the sin of Judas the betrayer is regarded as so heinous that he is forever confined to the core of an icy hell). And this is to begin to objectify these passages, for as worshippers of an ethical and just God, we ought at once to identify with every scream against injustice, either on our own behalf or (especially) on behalf of others. So the psalmist's lament can stand not only for his own personal experience, but for the cry of all who endure injustice in every age. And if we can identify with such a cry, we can also identify with the prayer that underlies it, which is that God may banish the sin and falsehood that compromise the world he has designed, and may re-establish justice in the earth.

It's important to remember that the imprecations are couched as prayers addressed to God, not as curses let loose on human beings. Throughout the laments, there is a strong notion of 'covenant' as a relationship of 'steadfast love' initiated by God towards Israel, in return for which Israel is to give back her loyal obedience. This kind of relationship mirrors treaties entered into in the ancient world whereby a powerful nation would offer 'protection' to a vassal state in return for its loyalty. Set out in the treaty document would be a series of blessings on the vassal if she complies, and curses if she fails to. One way, then, of reading the imprecations of the psalms is to see them as the curse inevitably brought down upon covenant-breakers who, by oppressing the poor rather than protecting them, violate the first principles of a justly ordered society.

We can recognize, too, that it is cathartic (that is, it 'cleanses' the spirit) to externalize outrage and hurl the language of curse into the skies in this way. Otherwise, we risk poisoning our souls with our own bitterness and hatred. This harbouring of a wish to curse is precisely what has happened to the enemy himself (17–18). As we have seen, the emotional and spiritual honesty of the Psalter is one of its greatest gifts. Whereas contemporary spirituality can easily collapse prayer into the thinking aloud of beautiful and pleasant thoughts, the Hebrew Bible is infinitely more realistic about human nature. Like the passionate anger of Jeremiah's laments and the sufferer's speeches in the Book of Job, the Psalms insist that true prayer must not pretend.

The offering of life to God is the offering of its shadow as well as its light. And if in that shadow there lurk wishes and desires that need to be forgiven, God will see to it.

We know that we live in a world where countless people continue to be the powerless victims of others' cruelty and inhumanity. These voiceless 'poor' have one recourse: to voice their protest as impassioned lament to the Almighty. It is often assumed that the imprecations of the Psalms are unsuitable for the worship of today's Church. But if they are one way in which the Church can stand alongside those who thirst for justice and truth, how can such psalms *not* find a place in prayer? But perhaps we need to do this with an uneasy conscience, aware of our propensity to be carried away by the rhetoric of imprecation. To recite psalms such as these while continuing to love our enemies as Jesus commands is a high spiritual challenge. But the psalmist himself acknowledges that love is the fundamental value he tries to live by (5). Is this how he sees divine blessing even in the midst of human curse (28)? If so, it is a rather wonderful foretaste of the gospel.

23

Maker and Deliverer

The Twenty-third Evening: Psalms 114, 115

This evening takes us to the very heart of Old Testament faith. Both tonight's psalms honour the God of Israel as supreme. In the first, YHWH is supreme over creation, for in delivering his people he has demonstrated his power over the forces of the natural world, both in the water and on land. In the second, he is supreme above all other 'gods', for whereas they are lifeless entities incapable of movement or activity, YHWH as LORD of heaven and earth is the source of all life who alone deserves a people's worship and obedience.

Psalm 114 is a hymn of the exodus. Many of the Psalms celebrate the deliverance of the Hebrews from their Egyptian slavery, for as we have already seen, the exodus was as central to Israel's faith as the cross and resurrection are to Christianity. Among the psalms of the exodus, Psalm 105 is notable as a jubilant recital of God's great acts of salvation. Psalm 114 is a distillation of that narrative. Its author is a gifted miniaturist, who in a mere fifty-two Hebrew words charmingly captures the spirit of this defining story and compels us to reverence the God who is its central character. This little psalm's winsome use of imagery suggests (though it's impossible to be certain) that it could belong to the very earliest tradition of how the exodus story was told, and maybe acted out in a liturgical ceremony of some kind.

It begins by stating the divine purpose of the exodus, which was to create a people dedicated to God. 'When Israel went out from Egypt, the house of Jacob from a people of strange language, Judah became his sanctuary, Israel his dominion' (1–2). So condensed is the language that the text doesn't explicitly mention God at this point (see the footnote in the NRSV here). To bring about a covenant community safe from threat and installed in their own land entailed overcoming huge natural obstacles. For the moment, the psalmist simply records the momentous events without explaining them: 'The sea looked and fled; Jordan turned back. The mountains skipped like rams, the hills like rams' (3–4). This delightful *poesie* refers to the crossing of both sea and river that marked the start and finish of the Exodus, and the difficult passage across the mountainous interior of Sinai in between. It has the effect of increasing the tension in the psalm: we want to know how this has come about.

So, the poet indulges in a playful catechism, quizzing the landscape itself: 'Why is it, O sea, that you flee? O Jordan, that you turn back? O mountains, that you skip like rams? O hills, like lambs?' (5–6). Cleverly, the final couplet refrains from answering these questions directly (which would be how a prose writer would deal with it). Instead, the response is given as a summons to the natural order to reverence the God who has performed these unforgettable works: 'Tremble, O earth, at the presence of the LORD!' (7–8). That is to say, the only possible response to the Exodus is to worship the God of Israel for his faithfulness. For if the earth is required to honour YHWH in this way, how much more must his people devote themselves to gratitude and praise?

The next psalm follows on seamlessly. *Psalm 115* probably comes from a later era than its predecessor, yet there is a natural connection of ideas. The opening act of praise could well have stood as the coda to Psalm 114: what more appropriate than, having heard the story of God's acts of history, to exclaim, 'Not unto us, O LORD, not unto us, but unto thy name give the praise!' (1, BCP). And since his control over the forces of nature has shown him to be the supreme Mover in the world, it follows that no other being can compare with him. No other god can do what YHWH does. His claim to be the absolute and unique sovereign of the universe is secure.

As in some laments we have studied already (such as Psalm 74.22), this psalm appeals to God to honour his own nature by pleading his cause in the face of rival claims to godhood. 'Why should the nations say, "Where is their God?"' (2). Perhaps there is silence in heaven at this point, for the psalmist answers for him: 'Our God is in the heavens; he does whatever he pleases' (3). This absolute claim is followed up by a ringing indictment of the deities who compete for divine status. They are dubbed 'idols', fabricated indeed out of precious metals and beautiful, even majestic, to look at but for all that no more than 'the work of human hands' (4). Accordingly their powers do not even equal those of the mortals who made them. 'They have mouths, and speak not: eyes have they, and see not' (5, BCP).

So far, so sarcastic. But the sting is in the tail of this tragicomic list of the attributes of powerlessness: 'Those who make them are like them' (8). The manufacturers of these *soi-disant* gods are as impotent as they are, a theme lovingly developed in Isaiah 44.9–20, where the prophet pours scorn on those who do not see the sheer illogic in ascribing divine power to objects of their own making. But what we don't perhaps expect is the psalmist's next remark: 'so are all who trust in them' (8). It's a devastating critique of idolatry, of a piece with the Bible's belief that we become like the god we worship. If we attach our values, our trust and our loyalty to what is essentially impotent, without any life of its own, that is how we shall end up – lifeless. This is hardly surprising, given the root meaning of the word 'worship' – to ascribe 'worth' to something or someone.

So, the consequence of all worship is that we inevitably imitate the object of our worship and desire. This psalm leaves worshippers of false gods without excuse. Even if they were beguiled or seduced into it, the evidence of their own lives ought to have called them back to reality. Idolatry is not simply bad for humans. It is fundamentally irrational; it doesn't make sense. What then is the thinking creature's response to the world? It's the threefold invitation to 'trust in the LORD!' (9–11), addressed not only to Israel but to all who fear him: 'He is their help and their shield.' For all the evidence points to a God who holds humanity in mind and is good to them: 'he will bless those who fear the LORD, both small and great' (12–13). In wisdom literature 'the fear of the LORD' is synonymous with wisdom (Job 28.28). Moreover, in later Jewish writing 'God-fearers' is a phrase often used of non-Jews who had opted to associate with the covenant community as worshippers of YHWH. So they, too, are the heirs of God's blessing on all who follow this wise and wholesome path to life: 'May you be blessed by the LORD, who made heaven and earth' (14–15).

The psalmist's reference to the act of creation leads to a final theological reflection on the nature of God. 'The heavens are the LORD's heavens, but the earth he has given to human beings' (16). This important statement takes us back to the psalm's opening. In contrast to idols who can do nothing, 'Our God is in the heavens; he does whatever he pleases' (3). Here again is an unambiguous assertion of monotheism: all other gods are discredited, and only YHWH is supreme over creation. (Compare Psalm 82 where the same conclusion is reached by a different route: we recall how there YHWH's supremacy was established on the grounds of his *ethical* and *moral* character.) There is an important understanding of the world in this key statement: here, as in Psalm 8 and the Genesis stories of creation, humanity as a whole (not just Israel) is 'given' the earth, not to exploit but to enjoy, and to take responsibility for its welfare on behalf of all other living things. So this world-affirming psalm ends with a hymn of gratitude for the privilege of being alive (17) and being able, therefore, to bless God for his goodness by singing a joyous alleluia (18, BCP).

In its attack on idols, this psalm has much in common with a number of passages in Isaiah 40–55, of which we have already quoted one example. Of course, Hebrew faith was relentlessly opposed to idolatry at every phase of its life, but this became a particularly sharp issue during the time of exile in Babylon in the sixth century BCE. This is the period during which the unnamed prophet whom we call the 'Second Isaiah' was preaching. His task was to recall the exiles to their historic faith in YHWH by establishing his supremacy as Creator over the Babylon deities they were tempted to worship. As the universal God of all things, his saving purposes would no longer be confined to Israel but would include the whole of humanity. Israel would be restored to her own land, and this new 'exodus' would lead to a wonderful manifestation of divine glory that all the world would see.

It's likely that the background of Psalm 115 is similar to that of Second Isaiah, perhaps coming from a time when the community had reason to think its exile would soon be over. If so, it speaks powerfully to people undergoing personal or communal ordeals of any kind. When the lamp of faith burns low, and it's tempting to resort to other sources of solace and distraction (whatever the 'idols' we have a propensity to give our 'worth' to), the God of Israel invites us to turn back to him. As the Creator and Mover of history, we find in him the strength we need to face our unknown futures. He is our source and life and end, as the exodus story taught the Hebrews (Psalm 115.12): 'The LORD has been mindful of us; he will bless us.' It will often not be clear how his purposes of good will be worked out; nevertheless faith rises above our perplexity, and issues in praise and thanksgiving: 'we will bless the LORD from this time on and for evermore' (18).

24

The way of happiness

The Twenty-fourth Evening: Psalm 119.1–32

———•◆•———

Psalm 119 is unique. Its great length, its elaborate architecture and its subject matter all mark it out as a composition without peer not only within the Psalter but in the entire Bible.

Its theme is set out in the first verse: 'Happy are those whose way is blameless, who walk in the law of the LORD.' This takes us right back to the opening lines of the Psalter. The very first psalm in the book strikes the same note of devotion to God's law, with the invitation to find in the study of the law lasting fulfilment. 'Happy are those who do not follow the advice of the wicked, or take the path that sinners tread, or sit in the seat of scoffers; but their delight is in the law of the LORD, and on his law they meditate day and night' (Psalm 1.1–2). The second part of Psalm 19 is very similar. But as both those psalms belong to the Morning cycle of the Prayer Book, 119 is the first time we have met this kind of content in the Evening Psalms.

What does the psalmist mean when he speaks about the 'law'? *Torah* is the name by which the first division of the Hebrew Scriptures, the five 'Books of Moses' or the 'Law' are known in the Jewish community. So it's tempting to think that these books are specifically what the psalmist has in mind. This is by no means impossible, for the psalm is admitted by all scholars to be one of the latest in the Psalter, and could come from an era when those five books of the

'Law' had acquired something like their final 'canonical' shape.

However, the Hebrew word *torah* literally means 'teaching' or 'instruction', which suggests a rather wider sense than simply the written text of 'law'. Throughout the psalm the writer exalts *torah* as the means by which he knows himself led and guided by God into the paths of goodness. His delight in *torah* is comparable to other psalmists' delight in the sanctuary or temple (Psalms 42/43, 84): what is uppermost in his mind is not so much the means as the end itself, which is nothing less than God's very presence which it is his will that human beings should enjoy. God is as real to this psalmist through *torah* as he is to the worshipper in the temple. It's not too much to say that in an era when temple worship was in decline, or, later, when the cult ceased for ever, *torah* came to substitute for it. It represented the same reality. God was present anywhere and everywhere his *torah* was honoured and embraced.

It's well known that this psalm mentions *torah* either explicitly or by way of one or more synonyms in almost every one of its 176 verses. Moreover, it employs no fewer than seven other different words to bring variety to the way it speaks about *torah* – 'precepts', 'testimonies' or 'decrees', 'commandments', 'statutes', 'judgments' or 'ordinances', 'promises' and, perhaps most simply and directly of all, 'word' or 'words': eight terms in all. It may or may not be a coincidence that the number eight lies at the basis of the psalm's structure. It consists of twenty-two sections, each one an octave of eight verses that begin with the same letter of the Hebrew alphabet from *aleph* to *taw*. We have met this acrostic 'A to Z' architecture before in some of the wisdom psalms (see Psalms 34 and 37).

'Wisdom' perhaps best describes this psalm, too, with its calm, measured 'take' on life that models so well a reflective response to its unpredictable changes and chances. Perhaps it features also in allusions to the instruction of the young (9). It's surely no accident that it seems especially to have been loved by St Benedict who in his *Rule for Monks* makes it a cornerstone of his provision for how the Psalter was to be recited in community each week. The Benedictine virtues of 'balance' and 'stability' are precisely what Psalm 119 is designed to inculcate. In the Judaism of the centuries after the exile, this meditative piety became more and more valued, whether in small gatherings of worshippers studying *torah*, or among individuals seeking to deepen their relationship with God by immersing themselves in divine instruction. In this, the written text of Scripture as the object of study and devotion came to play an increasingly central role.

In Cranmer's psalm cycle, Psalm 119 is allocated to three evenings and the two mornings in between. Thus the Twenty-fourth, Twenty-fifth and Twenty-sixth Evenings form a kind of three-day breather or retreat in the cycle, calmer seas amid the tides of more passionate praise and turbulent lament. There is really only one theme, as we have seen. In a way, the first verse says it all. There is no 'argument' to speak of, no progression from beginning to end. Yet the content never feels dull or repetitious; like Psalm 37, that single theme undergoes marvellously inventive permutations through its 176 variations. This gives the psalm its welcome, soothing quality. Yet the psalmist, like any human being, experiences times of distress and difficulty, and the psalm chronicles these (for example, 81–88): the seas are not always as smooth as they look.

The first four sections, *Psalm 119.1–32*, are introduced by a double *'ashre*, the lovely Hebrew word for 'happy' (1–2). 'Happy are those whose way is blameless, who walk in the law of the Lord. Happy are those who keep his decrees, who seek him with their whole heart.' It would be easy to read this as if it extolled virtue for its own sake. But it becomes clear even as the first four sections of the psalm unfold that happiness has deeper roots than simply living the good life, though choices about how to live are of course an aspect of it. These roots lie in the psalmist's relationship with God. 'I will praise you with an upright heart, when I learn your righteous ordinances . . . With my whole heart I seek you; do not let me stray from your commandments' (7–10). Indeed, it's striking that whereas the first three verses of the psalm are couched in the descriptive and impersonal third person 'happy are those' (just like Psalms 1 and 37), from then onwards the psalmist speaks to God directly: 'You have commanded your precepts to be kept diligently' (4). This highly personal form of address is prayer of a deeply intimate kind. This, surely, is where the psalmist's 'happiness' has its origins. There is, however, an undertow in these waters whose surface appears so untroubled. It's hinted at in these first sections. There are suggestions of shame (6, 31), abandonment (8), impurity (9), estrangement (19), persecution (21–23), humiliation (25), distress (28) and falsehood (29). While it isn't always clear how far some of these allusions may be intended as metaphors of longing and desire for God, they do connect this psalm with the language of the personal laments, and this becomes stronger as we travel through the psalm. Just as in the laments the answer to the psalmist's suffering was always to turn to God in the prayer of faith and hope with the expectation that one day he would offer thanksgiving in the sanctuary, it's very similar here. By meditating on God's teaching, a way through dark times is opened up and the path ahead is lit (105).

The Twenty-fourth Evening ends with a sentiment that beautifully sums up the thought of the psalm thus far. 'I run the way of your commandments, for you enlarge my understanding' (32). In the Hebrew it is 'heart' rather than 'mind' that the psalmist refers to: 'when thou hast set my heart at liberty' (BCP). The sense is that life lived in the fear and love of God is constantly expanding in its possibilities, for it is no longer hemmed in by fear or anxiety. For the psalmist, to immerse himself in divine *torah* is to be liberated from all that diminishes life. God's commandments are themselves life-giving and life-changing, and this makes them not a burden but a joy. To have the heart 'enlarged' is to begin to see how we might live not out of self-interest but out of generosity. And that is truly humanizing.

25

Stability

The Twenty-fifth Evening: Psalm 119.73–104

─•◆•─

In these four sections, *Psalm 119.73–104*, the psalmist's suffering has evidently not gone away. But he finds strength in the thought that not only has God 'made and fashioned me' (73) but his steadfast love and mercy are his comfort and support at all times (76–77). Anticipating deliverance, and meanwhile poring over God's *torah*, he invites others to come and learn the ways of God from him themselves: 'Let those who fear you turn to me, so that they may know your decrees' (79). The liberating effect of God's word on his life has become a matter not only of public evidence but also public testimony. It's not enough that others *see*: they also need to *know* and *understand* where this transformation comes from. The BCP is closer to the Hebrew here: 'O let my heart be sound in thy statutes: that I be not ashamed' (80). This is about the psalmist's integrity. Whether you look on the surface or to the inward life of the person, it's a consistent story of wholeness and truth.

The next octave is marked by an increased sense of urgency. There is a palpable unease here that is the closest this equable psalm comes to true lament. Each verse adds to the sense of threat: ' "When will you comfort me?" ' (82); 'I have become like a wineskin in the smoke' (83); 'They have almost made an end of me on earth' (87). Yet only once does he seem almost to cross the threshold of inward collapse, in a rare verse that does not mention *torah* at all: 'How long must your servant endure? When will you judge those who persecute me?' (84). In every other verse, the psalmist answers his own complaint by invoking God's statutes and ordinances. 'I hope in your word' (81); 'yet I have not forgotten your statutes' (83); 'All your commandments are enduring' (86); 'I have not forsaken your precepts' (87). This has the effect of stabilizing his spirit, as if *torah* were a kind of gyroscope. And even in his final, plaintive cry, 'In your steadfast love spare my life', it is only for the sake of honouring *torah*: 'so that I may keep the decrees of your mouth' (88).

What follows is the restoration of confidence. In contrast to the fickleness and malice of human beings, God's decrees are both everlastingly good and eternally trustworthy. 'O Lord, thy word: endureth for ever in heaven' (89, BCP). How does the psalmist know this? By considering the evidence around him, both in history and in the natural order. 'Your faithfulness endures to all generations; you have established the earth, and it stands fast' (90). As in all the wisdom literature, the wise man or woman is someone who is able to 'see into the life of things', as Wordsworth put it in one of his poems. He realizes that the stability of the world is the image he needs in order to re-establish his own stability. 'By your appointment they stand today, for all things are your servants. If your law had not been my delight, I would have perished in my misery' (91–92). So he vows never to forget the source of his life and flourishing, for he belongs entirely to God (93–94). And although the wicked still lurk with minds set on destruction (95), they no longer hold any fear. In the face of the world's transience and his own mortality, there is permanence in *torah* and this not only enables him to see things for what they are, but it also brings the hope he needs to live by. 'I see that all things come to an end: but thy commandment is exceeding broad' (96, BCP).

The final section of the Twenty-fifth Evening is the psalmist's response to his crisis of faith on the basis of *torah* as his answer to it. 'Oh, how I love your law! It is my meditation all day long' (97). His love for God's *torah* is so intense that he invokes a series of comparisons to express how it has irradiated his life. 'Your commandment makes me wiser than my enemies, for it is always with me' (98). No fearer of God would dispute that this is an indisputable effect of *torah* piety. But then the comparisons become more extreme. 'I have more understanding than all my teachers, for your decrees are my meditation. I understand more than the aged, for I keep your precepts' (99–100). This seems to fly in the face of the respect, constantly urged by wisdom writers, that is owed by the young towards their teachers and their elders. However, this is meant as hyperbole, albeit a particularly bold example of it. The point is that through *torah*, God himself is the psalmist's teacher, the one who alone imparts true wisdom: 'I do not turn away from your ordinances, for you have taught me' (102). So good is this teaching that it can only be compared to the best food he knows (103; cf. Psalm 19.10). Compared to the barren paths of falsehood (104), *torah* is the greatest delight the world affords.

26

A path for the wandering

The Twenty-sixth Evening: Psalm 119.145–176

———◆◆◆———

With *Psalm 119.145–176* we have reached the final sections of this long meditative poem. Because there is no linear argument, it would be misleading to call the last part of the psalm a conclusion, though there is a sense of quiet resolution towards the end. But while much of what the psalmist says under these four final letters of the alphabet recapitulates content from earlier in the poem, there is no flagging in his literary inventiveness in finding new ways to re-state old truths: the words and images are as fresh as they were two evenings ago.

There is another episode of restlessness in the first two sections (145–160). Those who are giving the psalmist grief have not gone away. Perhaps the psalmist, besieged by trouble, is sleepless and, as the wise have always done, he has learned how to turn insomnia first into vigilance and then prayer. 'I cry to you; save me . . . I rise before dawn and cry for help . . . My eyes are awake before each watch of the night' (146–148). Perhaps these are hours of prayer already decided upon in his mind. In any event, his plea for deliverance is more than merely self-protection. It is 'that I may meditate on your promise' (148). There is a nice play on images of distance here. While 'those who persecute me with evil purpose draw near', nevertheless 'they are far from your law. Yet you are near, O LORD, and all your commandments are true' (150–151). In *torah* there is a 'real presence'

149

close to the one who holds fast to God's word; for all his life the psalmist has known that God's decrees are trustworthy because they are 'established for ever' (152; cf. 89, 96).

Yet for a while, it seems that the psalmist's oft-stated 'delight' in *torah* has been eclipsed by his own suffering. 'Look on my misery and rescue me' (153). Like yesterday's section 81–88, the psalmist's distress looks ready to gain the upper hand. As in the laments, the psalmist looks to God to be his advocate and deliverer: 'Plead my cause and redeem me' (154). Yet while the shadows are never quite banished, this is the last time that the psalmist experiences the rush of anxiety and threat. And this episode is less long-lasting than previous ones. He knows that his persecutors cannot survive for long because 'they do not keep your commands' (158). By contrast, he is able confidently to pray: 'Consider how I love your precepts; preserve my life according to your steadfast love' (159). The ground of his assurance is the same as it was before: 'The sum of your word is truth; and every one of your righteous ordinances endures for ever' (160).

The next octave (161–168) begins as though the psalmist is going to continue his complaint. 'Princes persecute me without cause' (161). But this is in fact the last time that his oppressors are directly named. The antithesis to enmity is trust in divine *torah*: 'but my heart stands in awe of your words'. And this love of God's teaching remains the focus throughout this more serene section of the psalm. So precious is it that it is like buried treasure (162), an image taken up by Jesus in one of his parables of the kingdom (Matthew 13.44–46). For the psalmist it is truth (163), peace (165), salvation (166) and promise (168) all folded into one divine gift, so much to be cherished that it is the cause of his constant offering of praise: 'Seven times a day I praise you for your righteous ordinances' (164). This text was famously made the basis for the seven daily 'hours' of prayer by St Benedict in his *Rule for Monks*. But it's probably meant as spiritual hyperbole. 'Seven times a day' means 'all the time': for how could the psalmist not give himself to thanksgiving when every moment of every day is an opportunity to enjoy the gift without price of God's life-giving presence in *torah*?

The final section (169–176) draws together material from earlier in the psalm by offering it to the LORD. 'Let my cry come before you, O LORD . . . Let my supplication come before you' (169–170). Like the laments, his prayer moves from grief to joy, for he has the certainty that God will not only hear his complaint but will answer it; indeed, has already begun to do so. 'My lips will pour forth praise, because you teach me your statutes. My tongue will sing of your promise, for all your commandments are right' (171–172). But the psalmist is realistic about the nature of religious faith. His confidence must never be misplaced. Even in thankfulness, he remains utterly dependent on God for his life, welfare and happiness. So the shout of praise subsides into a more tentative prayer for God's saving, helping presence. 'Let your hand be ready to help me . . . I long for your salvation, O LORD . . . Let me live that I may praise you' (173–175).

The final verse of all is one of the most poignant not only in this psalm but in the entire Psalter. 'I have gone astray like a lost sheep; seek out your servant, for I do not forget your commandments' (176). We might expect such a long and troubled journey to end with a triumphant flourish, a shout of praise perhaps as in the previous few verses. But life remains fragile. The future is precarious. The enemy may be at bay for now, but the psalmist knows himself well enough to recognize that he has 'fightings within' as well as 'fears without', as the well-known hymn puts it (by the Victorian writer Charlotte Elliott, 'Just as I am without one plea').

Perhaps the true adversary is his own propensity to deviate from the way of *torah*, to try to find satisfaction or fulfilment other than in God's life-giving presence. The image of the poor wandering sheep that has strayed far from the path of safety and no longer hears the voice of the beloved shepherd touches us deeply not least through its links both to Psalm 23 and to the teaching of Jesus (Luke 15.3–7).

Such are all of us, urges the psalmist. For when everything has been said at such great length, when it has been probed, studied, explored, meditated on, prayed about, tried, tested and acted upon, it comes down to a very simple truth. With the presence of God to nourish and sustain us and the humane, generous way of *torah* to guide us, we have all that we need to become what we were meant to be as men and women. The purpose of our Creator and Redeemer is that we should be 'fully alive' – for this, as the early church father Irenaeus famously said, is the 'glory of God'. This is more than living wisely and responsibly in this world (a challenge enough). It has to do with being both contented and joyful as his children, finding true happiness in relationship with God without whom the world becomes a place of mirage and falsehood.

For the psalmist this is encapsulated in one of his favourite ideas, 'delight'. For him, delight in God's word is delight in God himself. The enjoyment of God is where obedient discipleship begins. Growth into a mature spirituality of *torah* delight is a long journey into a landscape that can be strange, even difficult and threatening. Perhaps the extreme length of this psalm is a kind of parable of this, as is the refusal to opt for some kind of easy closure in the final verse. For in his journey of faith, this psalmist is realistic about the possibility that even at the point where he nears its end, he could still lose his way, wandering away like a sheep without direction. 'Then I saw that there was a way to Hell even from the Gates of Heaven', says John Bunyan's

Pilgrim near the end of *Pilgrim's Progress*. The acute psychological insight and spiritual realism with which this psalm
ends demonstrates not only the stamina of this long psalm's
another, but also his wisdom.

27

On the ascent

The Twenty-seventh Evening:
Psalms 126, 127, 128, 129, 130, 131

——•◆•——

After the longest psalm in the book comes a sequence of fifteen short (some very short) psalms entitled in the Hebrew Bible 'Songs of Ascents'. This collection perhaps began as an anthology of songs sung by pilgrims 'going up' to Jerusalem for the festivals. The journey to the Temple was always seen as an 'ascent', not simply on account of the significance of the nation's focal city, but because arriving at Zion's hill-top site was a clear metaphor of spiritual 'ascent' into the presence of God himself. And while not all these psalms are obvious songs of pilgrimage, the theme of Zion as God's holy dwelling-place and source of blessing is explicit or implicit in many of them.

The six psalms that make up the Twenty-seventh Evening begin with a beautiful song of homecoming, which pilgrimage always is. *Psalm 126* celebrates the end of exile and the people's return to their beloved Zion. Whereas in Babylon they had been taunted by the captors to sing 'one of the songs of Zion', and had bemoaned the impossibility of singing 'the Lord's song in a strange land' (Psalm 137.1–4, BCP), once the Lord had 'restored the fortunes of Zion . . . our mouth was filled with laughter, and our tongue with shouts of joy' (1–2). In an earlier psalm, the observing nations had asked, 'Where is their God?' (Psalm 115.2). Now they know. 'The

LORD has done great things for them' (2). This is a story Israel needs to testify to for herself (3).

The sorrows of exile are not forgotten with the rapture of return, for the redemptive movement from tears to joy does not belong only to history. It's part of the annual cycle of the seasons. Every act of sowing and of reaping relives it: to sow is always an act of faith, for who is to know whether the winter rains will come and whether the LORD will continue to 'restore our fortunes' (4) through the gift of a fruitful harvest? So the prayer for the fertility of the land is a natural consequence of how God has given it back to his people. 'May those who sow in tears reap with shouts of joy' (5). The psalm ends with a shout that acclaims the sower's joyful homecoming with his harvest, as if he were a returning exile. And we are right to derive encouragement from this psalm in our own activity of planting and watering as we look to grow harvests of peace, truth and justice in the world. For when we have sowed in God's name with tears of longing, we must live in the hope that God will in time give the increase and with it, the joy of homecoming for all the human family.

Psalm 127 is inspired by thoughts of Zion where the pilgrim is headed. YHWH is its true architect and guardian: 'Unless the LORD builds the house, those who build it labour in vain. Unless the LORD guards the city, the guard keeps watch in vain' (1). As a pilgrim, the psalmist focuses first on the 'house' as the temple for the Davidic dynasty. But, on a long journey far away (presumably) from those he loves, his thoughts turn to his own 'house' both as home and as a personal 'dynasty' made up of his own precious children (3–5). The blessings of family life, then, are as God-given and God-protected as the blessings the pilgrim will receive from Zion and its sanctuary. And 'blessing' on home, family and daily work is not a matter of relentless activism and sleepless nights, 'the bread of anxious toil' (2). It comes with the gift of a restful spirit, confident in God's provision. Whether in our civic or personal life, this suggests a work ethic informed by divine blessing on the harvests of human endeavour, often beyond our dreams.

The theme of wholesome family life as a God-given harvest is continued into *Psalm 128*. Here is another wisdom *'ashre*: 'Happy is everyone who fears the LORD, who walks in his ways' (1). The gift that honours the psalmist's devotion to God is both that his labour will prosper, and that contentment will accompany it (2). But the decisive sign of God's blessing lies in his home and his family, and in a 'table' sufficient to provide for them (3). And in this he sees a picture of the wider 'family' of Israel blessed by her generous and gracious God. Just as the previous psalm began with Zion and ended in the home, so this psalm begins in the home and ends with the pilgrim's sights lifted to Jerusalem once more. For when Zion is the focus of prayer and longing, and when God blesses the people from there (5), their future flourishing is assured both as families and as a pilgrim nation: 'May you see your children's children. Peace be upon Israel!' (6).

The fourth psalm of the Evening continues to explore the themes of blessing and harvest, this time from the standpoint of those who have been troubled in the past. *Psalm 129* begins with a memory of the days when Israel was under attack. Yet the enemy did not prevail despite the wounds and the scars they left behind, recalled in a vivid agricultural image: 'Those who plough ploughed on my back; they made their furrows long' (1–3). Perhaps this reminds worshippers of their ancestors' slavery in Egypt; perhaps a more recent ordeal is in mind, exile perhaps, like Psalm 126. But such hostile 'ploughing' is of no avail in Zion, for God 'has cut the cords of the wicked' (4). The fruits of these futile assaults of the enemy are contrasted with the bulging sheaves of the righteous in Psalm 126: they are as ephemeral as withered grass on a housetop (6–7). And whereas in the previous psalm the righteous inherit the blessing of Zion (Psalm 128.5), in this psalm blessing is withheld from those who hate Zion (8); for them only shame and destruction awaits (5, 6). Psalm 129 then is the 'shadow' of 128. That psalm spelled out the happy consequences of being friends with God, this one the baleful outcome of setting oneself up as his enemy.

After a psalm about alienation from God, *Psalm 130* aptly charts the sinner's return to the LORD. *De Profundis* is one of the best known and cherished of the 'penitential psalms'. This personal lament begins where Psalm 129 left off, in the place where blessing is withheld: 'Out of the deep have I called unto thee, O LORD: LORD, hear my voice' (1, BCP). Overwhelmed by the chaotic waters that mirror (or stand for) the spiritual chaos within, the psalmist prays for restoration and in another vivid metaphor of longing for deliverance, keeps vigil through the night like 'those who watch for the morning' (6; we recall that the same image featured in one of the more agitated sections of Psalm 119.147–148).

But it is not simply a matter of watching and waiting. The psalmist must move towards God and acknowledge the reality of his state. To quote another of the evening penitential psalms, 'I said, "I will confess my transgressions to the LORD," and you forgave the guilt of my sin' (Psalm 32.5). Psalm 130's psalmist accepts that premise: 'If you, O LORD, should mark iniquities, LORD, who could stand? But there is forgiveness with you, so that you may be revered' (3–4). We may safely assume that between verses 4 and 5, the psalmist pours out his confession. Perhaps there are no *words* of contrition here because it is too deep for words: it is what is *felt* that is chronicled here, and in the 'depths' of the first line of this psalm, there is a world of confusion and lostness that words could never adequately express.

However, the day eventually breaks and the shadows disperse. The lament dissolves into a confidence in God that is as radiant as any in the Psalms: 'O Israel, hope in the LORD! For with the LORD there is steadfast love, and with him is great power to redeem' (7). There is no sin that is beyond the capacity of a loving God to forgive and heal (4, 8). And this is why the psalmist cries out to God in the first place, because he already knows that the 'forgiveness of sins' is an article of his faith. For it was the *hesed* of verse 7, God's 'covenant love', that all along motivated him to prayer and penitence. Confession is good for the soul because it is generated not by fear but by love. If guilt drives the soul into the arms of a merciful God, then the psalm is right to make so much of it. For while the truth about our condition is hard to bear, that truth is ultimately a kindness. Indeed, to find forgiveness 'so that you may be revered' (4) is to inherit the blessing, as an earlier psalm has already reminded us: 'Happy is everyone who fears the LORD, who walks in his ways' (128.1). Psalm 130 takes us right to the heart of the gospel.

After the turbulence of Psalm 130, *Psalm 131* offers peaceful resolution. The dreadful experience of chaos had destabilized the psalmist. It exposed the truth about sin, and that was humbling. So now, the psalmist knows how to be before God. 'O LORD, I am not high-minded: I have no proud looks. I do not exercise myself in great matters: which are too high for me' (1, BCP). This reminds us of the king promising not to tolerate 'a haughty look and an arrogant heart' (Psalm 101.5); only now, it is the psalmist who is being spoken about. 'But I have calmed and quieted my soul, like a weaned child with its mother' (2). This gentle image is unusually tender for the Psalms. We shouldn't assume too quickly that it's the child's point of view we glimpse here. It could well be the mother's, for what could be more restful or contented than for a mother to have her beloved child lying peacefully by her side? If so, this is one psalm that could plausibly have been written by a woman. It's not inconceivable that it shares its authorship with its predecessor from which it flows so naturally, not least in the line they both have in common, 'O Israel, hope in the LORD.'

28

Pain and mercy

The Twenty-eighth Evening:
Psalms 136, 137, 138

--- ◆ ---

The arithmetic of dividing the Psalter up into sixty portions
to provide psalms for the Morning and Evening services of
the month can lead to some odd juxtapositions. We have
already negotiated some interesting journeys where the sequence of psalms appointed for the evening either notice-
ably lightens (the Fourth and Sixteenth Evenings) or darkens
(the Ninth Evening). The Twenty-eighth Evening, however,
is in a class of its own among the Evening psalms. It begins
and ends with psalms that are among the most celebratory
and confident of any. Sandwiched between them is one of
the Psalter's bitterest laments. The abrupt change of mood
from thanksgiving to despair and then back to thanksgiving
again seems disconcerting, a sudden and unwelcome intru-
sion of a minor key when the tone has been so decisively set
in the major.

However, this emotional and spiritual bipolarity reflects
not only how the entire Psalter is, but even how individual
psalms are. A near neighbour, Morning Psalm 139, is a case
in point. Semitic cultures are not carefully modulated like
those of western Europe: rather, they express themselves
forcibly in absolutes and extremes. T. E. Lawrence 'of Arabia'
has a telling comment in *The Seven Pillars of Wisdom* about
how strange he found the concrete speech and thought of
the Arabs among whom he lived during the Great War: 'They

did not understand our metaphysical difficulties, our intro-spective questionings. They knew only truth and untruth, belief and unbelief, without our hesitating retinue of finer shades' (cited in G. B. Caird, *The Language and Imagery of the Bible*, 1980, p. 110). And if we let these three psalms stand alongside one another, disparate though they are, important insights emerge.

Psalm 136 is a litany of praise. We can imagine it sung antiphonally at ceremonies in the sanctuary, with singers responding to each bidding: 'for his steadfast love endures for ever'. This liturgical response consist of just three words in the Hebrew, the last of which is the now familiar *hesed*, God's covenant mercy towards his chosen people of Israel. The opening section (1–9) is a thanksgiving for creation, recalling the narrative with which the Hebrew Bible begins (Genesis 1). Then, however, the psalmist suddenly leaps from the celebration of the cosmos (9) to a detailed recital of Israel's saving history, the deliverance of the Hebrews from their Egyptian bondage (10–25). The connection is clear: a divinely ordered cosmos is of a piece with a divinely ordered history of salvation, and the establishment of a divinely ordered society that is loyal to the covenant, what the Psalter calls 'his servant Israel'. Having praised YHWH for his mighty acts of creation and redemption, the psalm ends where it began, by giving thanks to the God 'of heaven' whose covenant love is as sure as the sun and the stars.

The psalm's central affirmation is that God has raised up and delivered his people in their abasement. This same theme of exaltation is taken up in *Psalm 138*. This psalm is an individual thanksgiving for God's help and deliverance. Like Psalm 136, the theme is God's *hesed* or 'steadfast love' (2), which the psalmist has personally experienced through having cried out to God for help, and having been heard: 'on the day I called, you answered me' (3). The Hebrew Bible is insistent that God hears the cry of the weak and the poor who are, in a sense, his special treasure. Indeed, it is a mark of YHWH's being truly a god that he pays attention to those who are most in need, an issue made much of in Psalm 82, as have seen. Furthermore, our psalm celebrates how this God is in the habit of reversing human fortunes: 'though the LORD is high, he regards the lowly; but the haughty he perceives from far away' (6). This is precisely the theme of Mary's song, the *Magnificat*, a hymn that is no doubt modelled on psalms such as this: 'He hath put down the mighty from their seat, and hath exalted the humble and meek' (Luke 1.52, BCP). So while Psalm 136 is a communal act of praise, and 138 an individual's prayer of thankfulness, it is the appeal to thankfulness with which both psalms begin: 'O give thanks to the LORD, for he is good'; 'I give you thanks, O LORD, with my whole heart'.

Between these twin peaks of celebration, *Psalm 137* feels like the valley of the shadow of death. That it is one of the best-known psalms of all does not take away its sense of desperation. 'By the waters of Babylon we sat down and wept: when we remembered thee, O Sion' (1, BCP). Here, in the distant land of exile, psalmody is silenced, for how can exiles 'sing the LORD's song in a strange land?' (4, BCP). The forlorn abandonment of a vanquished people is palpable. We have already met it in Psalms 74 and 89, but here the pain feels more personal, more poignant. Who can forget the image of harps hung up on the willows whose weeping echoes the tears of exiles? Or the passionate curse they invoke upon themselves in case they should not hold their homeland constantly in their minds: 'If I forget you, O Jerusalem, let my right hand wither! Let my tongue cling to the roof of my mouth, if I do not remember you, if I do not set Jerusalem above my highest joy' (5–6).

But it is not only on the exiles themselves that imprecations are heaped, should they forget Zion. 'Happy shall they be who take your little ones and dash them against the rock!'

(9) continues the Psalm. Universally in the Psalter, the 'happiness' formula is applied to those who walk in God's way, as in the saying with which the book opens. Here, it is uncomfortable to say the least to have to recognize that it belongs to those who exact vengeance on the oppressor's infants. We have already encountered the psalmist's fierce explosions of rage against 'the enemy' in other psalms (such as Psalms 55, 69, 109) and have tried to suggest that these outbursts must be understood as part of the psalmist's prayer for a restoration of God's justice or right order in the world. This seems to be the thrust of the word that introduces the psalm's violent ending: 'Remember' (7). The importance of memory has already been established in the psalm's opening line, 'when we remembered Zion', and in the vow never to 'forget' Jerusalem. So, experience and vow are elevated into the prayer that God himself may 'remember' the plight of his people and act accordingly.

And this is the thread that connects the three psalms of the Twenty-eighth Evening. The first of the trio recalls how God has 'remembered us in our low estate . . . and rescued us from our foes' (136.23, 24). The last ends with the plea, 'Do not forsake the work of your hands' (138.8). In the lament they frame it is precisely the same people in sorrow and need who now cry out to God for help, as if Psalm 137 is a worked example or case study of the redemptive truth celebrated in the other two psalms. And like most laments, Psalm 137 is premised on the clear confidence of the psalmist that God will hear, even if it takes the form not of the quiet trustful prayer of thankfulness but the deafening scream of defiance. But that such a prayer is possible at all at a time like this indicates the psalmist's belief in a God who, as the *Magnificat* puts it, 'has helped his servant Israel, in remembrance of his mercy' (Luke 1.54).

It would be hard to exaggerate the importance of remembering in the Judaeo-Christian tradition. The Jewish

163

Passover is the celebration of a community's memory of deliverance, and indeed Psalm 136, an incomparable recital of the mighty acts of God known to Judaism as the Great Hallel, may have its origins in precisely this festival. In the same way, in the Christian Eucharist the Church makes present and explicit her memory of how God has delivered and saved the world in the coming of Jesus Christ. The great word of the institution of the Last Supper, *anamnesis*, means not simply telling a glorious story about the past, but making that past live in the present, actualizing it so that it becomes a powerful, life-changing force for the future. And this cannot mean remembering selectively. For Judaism, the bitterness of Egypt, and for Christianity, the darkness of Good Friday, are as central to memory as the new life that sprang from them.

So this trio of psalms reminds us of the need to hold together both the light and the shadow that are embedded in our memory, the memory of pain in Psalm 137 and the memory of mercy in Psalms 136 and 138. But perhaps it's significant that it is the psalm of lament that is book-ended by psalms of praise. *Eucharistia* means 'thanksgiving'. And to practise thankfulness at all times, whether in sorrow or gladness, happiness or pain, is the true goal of authentic spirituality.

29

Answer me quickly

The Twenty-ninth Evening: Psalms 142, 143

———•◦•———

This is the shortest Evening of the month, a mere 19 verses compared to the 73 of the longest. The Evening cycle began with two laments (Psalms 6 and 7) and now, almost at the end of the month, we are given the last two laments in the Psalms, for the rest of the Psalter is praise.

These two psalms are similar, and take up one more time many of the themes we have already met in the personal laments. The psalmist's distress is severe and is spoken of in the same image of abasement: in the first psalm he is 'brought very low' (142.6); in the second, his life is crushed 'to the ground, making me sit in darkness like those long dead' (143.3). In both, because the enemy is so powerful, there is an urgent plea for help before it is too late. And while both laments end with the psalmist's faith intact, the tone is hardly the most confident. We sense the fragility of his hope, as if it could fail at any moment.

Psalm 142 is particularly bleak. It begins with the psalmist's prayer for help. The repeated 'with my voice' (1), the piled up verbs of petition, 'I cry to the LORD . . . I make supplication . . . I pour out my complaint . . . I tell my trouble', reinforce the sense of utter destitution in which he finds himself. With a feeble gasp of faith, he is able to acknowledge that, 'When my spirit is faint, you know my way' (3), though this path is beset with snares, for the enemy is everywhere and in facing these threats he is entirely on his own

165

(4). So he cries out to YHWH: ' "You are my refuge, my portion in the land of the living" ' (5). As God is his only strength and protection (see Psalm 18), he begs to be delivered from his persecutors. For released from his (probably metaphorical) prison (6–7), he will once again praise God in the sanctuary, in the company of the righteous, where he will be surrounded by all that is safe and good and life-giving (7).

The last lament of the cycle, *Psalm 143*, is also the last of the penitential psalms. Not for the first time, it's not possible to be specific about the psalmist's ordeal, though the enemies who featured in the first lament (Psalm 6, the first penitential psalm) are still giving trouble here. Like Psalm 130, the opening prayer appeals to God not to deal with human beings according to what they deserve: 'Enter not into judgment with thy servant: for in thy sight shall no man living be justified' (2, BCP). Is the implication that the psalmist has been afflicted by way of punishment? Yet, despite the onslaughts of the enemy (3) and their crushing effect on the psalmist's inner life (4), he is able to summon up what in the circumstances is a magnificent effort of faith. Like Psalm 74, it is the memory of God's past deeds that sustains him: 'I remember the days of old, I think about all your deeds, I meditate on the works of your hands' (5). It feels like a faith that has to be fought for. Yet it is enough for the plea for mercy he needs to make: 'I stretch out my hands to you; my soul thirsts for you like a parched land' (6).

The second half of the psalm elaborates on this prayer. It appeals to God to act swiftly, for if he hides his face, 'I shall be like those who go down to the Pit' (7). This is the shadowy place of destruction, another way of speaking about Sheol where the dead were believed to descend. For when God turns his face away, it's as if life itself is taken. So the psalmist, again recalling Psalm 130, looks through the night of suffering to a morning of steadfast love, 'for in you I put my trust' (8). As a token of his seriousness, he pledges to walk in the path God sets before him: 'Teach me the way I should go, for to you I lift up my soul' (8). This sounds as though the psalm is going to end on a note of resolution. But this is not the case. Twice more the cry of distress punctures the psalmist's attempt to find some kind of stability (9, 11). Indeed, so desperate has he become by the end that the plea for help turns into a last outburst against the enemy itself with a plaintive whisper of acceptance to end with: 'In your steadfast love cut off my enemies, and destroy all my adversaries, for I am your servant' (12).

The unfinished business of this psalm makes for a thought-provoking tailpiece to the long series of laments we have travelled through during the monthly cycle. It's true that the Thirtieth and last evening of the month is undiluted joy, its psalms echoing the Christian affirmation that in the power of the resurrection, ' "Death has been swallowed up in victory . . . Where, O death, is your sting?" ' (1 Corinthians 15.54–55). Yet even amid the ecstatic celebration of praise, the Twenty-ninth Evening lingers on in the memory as a reminder of the pain and suffering that belong to the human state.

And this is necessary, for nothing is more callous to the suffering than that we should 'rejoice forgetfully', as if we could praise God with trumpets and cymbals (Psalm 150) while neglecting the pain of his world. That would be naked triumphalism, a propensity from which the Church is by no means immune and which it must always resist. We have already quoted the beautiful prayer of the Orthodox funeral rite with its profound instinct for Easter: 'even at the grave we sing alleluia'. But its obverse is just as true, and as spiritually and pastorally important: even as we sing alleluia, we are at the graveside with those who know the pain of the world and the tears of things.

Indeed, tomorrow's psalms of glory do not forget how God stands by those who are poor and needy, who are bowed under the weight of oppression and cruelty and have no hope to live for but YHWH himself. It's poignant that the Thirtieth Evening remembers in its opening hymn of praise the suffering of our two laments, how 'he gathers the outcasts of Israel. He heals the broken-hearted, and binds up their wounds . . . The LORD lifts up the downtrodden; he casts the wicked to the ground' (147.2–3, 6). Like the wounds of the risen and ascended Christ, humanity bears the marks of nails. These psalms don't yet achieve transfiguration. But they have the courage and the faith to pray for it; for in YHWH's covenant love (143.12), anything is possible.

30

Alleluia!

The Thirtieth Evening:
Psalms 147, 148, 149, 150

—◆•◆•◆—

The Prayer Book cycle has introduced us to psalms reflecting every conceivable situation. The interplay of light and shadow, lament and praise, passion and serenity is a mirror of what it is to be human. We have seen how sharply contrasting psalms are frequently juxtaposed in the Psalter (such as on the First, Ninth or Twenty-eighth Evenings) in ways that were not perhaps intended by those who first sang or wrote them. The effect can be arresting; for, compiled in a book that has its own shape and logic, their placing alongside one another accurately reflects the ebbs and flows of life that are familiar to every community and individual. Most of the Evenings of the month are an alchemy of different spiritual experiences, and this is part of the richness of reading the Psalms as a continuous cycle.

The Psalter does not begin with a blaze of trumpets but it ends with one (Psalm 150.3). All five final psalms begin with the shout *alleluia!*, literally, praise 'Yah' or YHWH. And this evening's quartet of joy is introduced by the words: 'How good it is to sing praises to our God; for he is gracious, and a song of praise is fitting' (Psalm 147.1). That could stand as a definition of psalmody, for a 'psalm' as we have seen is a song of praise. So, while lament in the presence of a compassionate God is both natural and right, the offering of praise is the fundamental response of faith. Lament is only possible because the psalmist already believes that God is good. Prayer only makes sense if we acknowledge that God's purposes for the universe and for his children are ultimately beneficent. So it's proper that the Psalter concludes with what is really an extended doxology, a catena of praise that gathers up and offers all that has been lived through in the journey through the book.

Psalm 147 is not the first psalm to link God's saving acts towards his people with his marvellous power in creation (for example, Psalm 136). Here, it's the restoration of the people to their own land that is the occasion for praise. 'The LORD builds up Jerusalem; he gathers the outcasts of Israel' (2); 'Praise your God, O Zion! For he strengthens the bars of your gates; he blesses your children within you. He grants peace within your borders' (12–14). This probably refers to the return from exile towards the end of the sixth century BCE. And this is of a piece with the grand sweep of his activity in the universe as a whole reminiscent of Psalm 104 and as beautifully declared. His control over the stars (4), the storms, snows, winds and rains (8, 16–18), his care for the earth's fertility (8), his generous provision for living things (9) are evidence to the psalmist of how divine power is used, not capriciously but for the good of creation. And Israel knows that this same power has led to her own deliverance.

But power, even the power that creates the universe, is not some naked energy or force, even when it results in the overthrow of the enemy (6). It is *ethical* in its exercise and outcomes, because this is how God himself is, and moral order pervades the kind of universe he has created. So a delivered people must live consistently with their experience of this morally executed power. 'His delight is not in the strength of the horse, nor his pleasure in the speed of a runner; but the LORD takes pleasure in those who fear him, in those who hope in his steadfast love' (10–11). And in a striking echo of Genesis 1 and Psalm 33.6, the same 'word' that God sends out to order the seasons and govern the world (15, 18) is also the 'word' by which Israel must live: 'He declares his word to Jacob, his statutes and ordinances to Israel' (19). This is what marks out Israel from all other peoples, that they have been given 'ordinances' as a rule of life to guide them (20; cf. Psalm 119). And this is where the psalm ends: with another *alleluia* of praise in the God whose purpose is realized not only in creation or in the welfare of his people, but (and we might say especially) in the obedient hearts and minds of those who love him.

In Psalm 147, creation is evidence of God's power, and human beings are invited to praise him. In the next psalm, creation leads the hymn of praise itself. Here, God's specific care of Israel has receded to the final verse, for the psalmist's focus is now nothing less than the panoply of creation itself. Eight times in its first few verses, *Psalm 148* summons the heavenly array to praise the LORD: the heavens with their angelic hosts; the sun, moon and stars, the waters above the skies must all take their part in this triumphant cosmic liturgy of celebration (1–6). 'Let them praise the name of the LORD, for he commanded and they were created' (5). The summons then turns from 'above' to 'below': the earth, the sea monsters, the depths, the seasons, animal and plant life (7–10). All these, too, must 'praise the LORD'.

Following the order of creation set out in the first chapter of Genesis, which moves from the skies to the earth and seas, then to the flora and fauna, finally reaching the apex of creation in the man and the woman made in God's own image (see also Psalm 8), our psalm finally reaches the world of human beings. No one is too exalted or lowly, wise or foolish, old or young to praise their Maker: 'Kings of the earth and all peoples, princes and all rulers of the earth! Young men and women alike, old and young together! Let them praise the name of the LORD' (11–13). Why? Because 'his name alone is exalted; his glory is above earth and heaven' (13). But why especially? Because 'He has raised up a horn for his people . . . for the people of Israel who are close to him' (14). In other words, Israel is privileged to be intimate with the Sovereign of the universe. This awesome thought, so artlessly dropped into the psalm right at the very end, deservedly earns another *alleluia*.

Psalm 149 is the Psalter's 'Magnificat'. Like the Song of Mary (Luke 1.46–55), it tells of how God has 'put down the mighty from their thrones, and has exalted the humble and meek'. Its opening *alleluia* is addressed to the 'faithful' or pious ones (*hasidim*), those who have understood that the paths of the LORD are all that is worth living for (1). So Israel is invited to sing, dance and make merry in honour of the Creator and King (2–3), 'for the LORD takes pleasure in his people' (4). But the focus is specific. It's the 'humble' who are adorned with victory; the 'faithful' who exult in glory (5). It's these unlikely 'saints' (as the Prayer Book version has it) whose praise of God gives them the instrument of victory (6). So the hostile nations are punished (7) and their high officers brought low (8), for this is the final vindication not only of God's people but of God himself (9).

The psalms of the last Evening get shorter and shorter, as if human speech with its shortcomings can no longer do justice to the majesty of God and his wonderful works. It's as if language needs to dissolve into a final act of praise and then lapse into silence because all that can ever be said has been said.

Psalm 150 is one of the most obviously 'cultic' of the Psalms, referring throughout to the worship of the temple. It begins with the invitation to 'praise God in his sanctuary' (1) and the summons to exploit every musical aid to do so: trumpet, lute, harp, tambourine, strings, pipe, cymbals – everything that makes a noise is to have its place in the orchestra of worship. But this symphony, played *fortissimo*, is no more than an echo of the cosmic hymn breathed at all times by all living things whether they know it or not (6); and the sanctuary is only a poor image of the vast 'firmament' of the heaven itself (1). It's as if the psalmist is saying: don't think so much of *initiating* your song of praise as joining in the eternal hymn that has been sung since time immemorial and will forever go on rising in a glorious crescendo of adoration, love and praise.

* * * *

With this powerful doxology, the Psalter comes to its grand climax. It utters its final *alleluia*, and dies away into silence. Yet its reverberations ring on eternally. And the pages that follow Psalm 150 are not empty. They are for us to write in, for this is where we take up the song for ourselves as the psalm itself has invited us to, and to keep alive the great tradition of psalmody in our own time as men and women of Israel's God. We do this by making the insights of the Psalter our own, by living and breathing its rhythms of praise and prayer, and by allowing the tides of our own sorrow and joy to be interpreted by it.

Above all, we do it by endeavouring to live faithfully in grateful response to the covenant of love we have been called into by the grace and *hesed*-mercy of God. And when life is done and it is time to gather up the fragments, we can dare to pray that whatever the pain we have endured and the forgiveness we need to ask for, our last word will be the one which the Book of Psalms sings out at the end of its long journey: ALLELUIA!

Suggestions for further reading

There are books without number on the Psalms, ranging from popular introductions to technical commentaries. The following is a small selection of books I have found valuable both for study and in teaching and spiritual guidance. The list includes some of the classics of psalm scholarship as well as more accessible texts for the ordinary reader (the latter are marked with an asterisk). Bible dictionaries and single volume commentaries (such as the *Oxford Bible Commentary*) will frequently be a useful and handy resource as will certain internet sites.

General background and introduction

Alter, Robert, *The Art of Biblical Poetry*, Edinburgh: T & T Clark, 1985.

Brown, William P., *Seeing the Psalms: A Theology of Metaphor*, Louisville: Westminster John Knox Press, 2002.

Crenshaw, James L., *The Psalms: An Introduction*, Grand Rapids: William B. Eerdmans, 2001.

Magonet, Jonathan, *A Rabbi Reads the Psalms*, London: SCM Press, 1994.

Mays, James L., *The LORD Reigns: A Theological Handbook to the Psalms*, Louisville: Westminster John Knox Press, 1994.

Mowinckel, Sigmund, *The Psalms in Israel's Worship*, ET, Oxford: Blackwell, 1962.

Ringgren, Helmer, *The Faith of the Psalmists*, London: SCM Press, 1963.

Commentaries

*Curtis, Adrian, *Psalms*, Epworth Commentaries, Peterborough: Epworth Press, 2004.

Dahood, Mitchell, *The Psalms*, Anchor Bible Commentary, 3 vols, New York: Doubleday, 1966, 1968, 1970.

Suggestions for further reading

Davidson, Robert, *The Vitality of Worship: A Commentary on the Book of Psalms*, Grand Rapids: W. B. Eerdmans, 1998.
*Eaton, John, *The Psalms: A Historical and Spiritual Commentary*, London, 2003.
*Kidner, Derek, *The Psalms*, Tyndale Old Testament Commentaries, 2 vols, Leicester: InterVarsity Press, 1973, 1975.
Weiser, Artur, *The Psalms*, ET, London: SCM Press, 1962.

Liturgy, Spirituality, and Life

Attridge, Harold W. and Fassler, Margot E., *Psalms in Community: Jewish and Christian Textual, Liturgical and Artistic Traditions*, Atlanta: Society of Biblical Literature, 2003.
*Box, Reginald, *Make Music to our God: How We Sing the Psalms*, London: SPCK, 1996.
Brown, Sally A. and Miller, Patrick D., eds, *Lament: Reclaiming Practices in Pulpit, Pew and Public Square*, Louisville: Westminster John Knox Press, 2005.
*Brueggemann, Walter, *Praying the Psalms*, Winona: St Mary's Press, 1986.
Brueggemann, Walter, ed. Miller, Patrick D., *The Psalms and the Life of Faith*, Augsburg: Fortress Press, 1995.
Gelston, Anthony, *The Psalms in Christian Worship: Patristic Precedent and Anglican Practice*, London: Alcuin Club and Group for Renewal of Worship, 2008.
Guiver, George, *Company of Voices: Daily Prayer and the People of God*, London: SPCK, 1988.
Lamb, J. A., *The Psalms in Christian Worship*, London: Faith Press, 1962.
*Lewis, C. S., *Reflections on the Psalms* (new edn), London: Fount, 1998.
*Mursell, Gordon, *Out of the Deep: Prayer as Protest*, London: Darton, Longman & Todd, 1989.
*Prothero, Rowland, *The Psalms in Human Life*, London: J. Murray, 1905.
Reid, Stephen Breck, ed., *Psalms and Practice: Worship, Virtue and Authority*, Collegeville: Liturgical Press, 2001.
*Rogerson, John, *The Psalms in Daily Life*, London: SPCK, 2001.
*Ryrie, Alexander, *Deliver Us from Evil: Reading the Psalms as Poetry*, London: Darton, Longman & Todd, 2004.

Suggestions for further reading

Stuhlmueller, Carroll, Demsey, Carol J. and Lenchak, Timothy A., *The Spirituality of the Psalms*, Collegeville: Liturgical Press, 2002.

Watson, J. R., *The English Hymn: A Critical and Historical Study*, Oxford: Clarendon Press, 1999, chapters 3–6.